You are
against Him. On this, there
is no neutrality.

2 Cor. 4:16-18

Isa. 40:31

Phil. 3:13

Jer. 33:3

Psalm 46:1

Mark 9:23
10:10:27

Blessings,

Yanger

Growing Up

Second Edition

Troy Langos

Edited by Glenn Pettit

author**HOUSE**®

AuthorHouse™
1663 Liberty Drive
Bloomington, IN 47403
www.authorhouse.com
Phone: 1-800-839-8640

Published by AuthorHouse 5/17/2012

ISBN: 978-1-4389-8739-2 (sc)
ISBN: 978-1-4389-8740-8 (e)

Contents

Preface

The first and foremost ingredient of growing up as a child of God is to feed on the Word of God daily and develop that intimate relationship with God as our Abba ~ Father. It is an absolute dependence on Him just as a child leans on his / her dad. One will never discover a meaning in life without instilling one's mind with God's truth. As it is written in Psalm 119: 105 *'Your word is a lamp to my feet And a light to my path,'* which articulates this fact.

The second phase of growing up is getting into the real battle field where one experiences God's presence and His Hand upon one's life through situations that come about in your life through people, failures, mistakes, defeats and victories. These situations make us to realize how weak and lonely we are without Christ. It is through this phase of breaking, molding and melting we get to the point where we know we are not on our own. There is someone in control of our lives and that is God Himself who created this universe for us to live in.

Suffering plays a major role in our growing up as Christians. This is a bitter truth to admit. Suffering is one of the ways that God shapes us and molds us to His likeness. To suffer in itself is not the point; it is what it does to us. It somehow hollows us out and on the other hand ripens us. No one really knows what is going on in the soul of an afflicted person with the inner ripening that takes place through the process of suffering and pain. All we know is God is Sovereign; He is Almighty, Amazing and Awesome. When we go through pain and sorrow, the presence of God, like a warm comforting blanket, can shield us, protect us, and allow the deep inner joy to surface even in the most devastating circumstances.

It is amazing to see the work suffering does when we don't let our trials go to waste and our pains go in vain. Apparently they shape us and make us into people who are a true reflection of Jesus Christ. Our pain can take us to the highest level of understanding who God is. Pain and trials are infernos by which our soul is forged. Troy's life is a powerful example of a man fighting a fierce battle in a real scenario of spiritual warfare. It gives me great joy and encouragement to see him grow day by day to what God wants him to be even though he faces pain and trials. I encourage and pray blessing for every reader that this book will accomplish God's purpose to help you grow more and more in Him even though you may be experiencing the worst patch of your life. Knowing that there is hope in His everlasting promises in Christ our Lord. Our hope is not in the present but in the things that are not seen and a future that is ordained by God.

But those who wait on the LORD
shall renew their strength;
They shall mount up with wings like eagles,
They shall run and not be weary,
They shall walk and not faint.
[Isaiah 40: 31 NKJV]

Maureena Prakash

Foreword

If we claim to have fellowship with him yet walk in the darkness, we lie and do not live by the truth. – 1 John 1:6

If anyone considers himself religious and yet does not keep a tight rein on his tongue, he deceives himself and his religion is worthless. – James 1:26

You believe that there is one God. Good! Even the demons believe that – and shudder. – James 2:19

Most of my life I deceived myself by thinking that I was Godly because I was a "good kid." I did not drink or do drugs growing up and I was not promiscuous. The passages cited above from 1 John 1:6 and James 1:26 describe the spiritual journey that I was on for the majority of my life, and James 2:19 describes the relationship that many of my friends have had with God Almighty. I was once a nominal Christian and I think that most "Christians" still are.

In my professional life as a high school teacher, I had the pleasure of working with professors from the University of Iowa, India University, and the University of Georgia to help teachers from several former Soviet Union countries write a democratic Social Studies curriculum. I helped teachers from Armenia, Moldova, Ukraine, Kyrgyzstan, and the Republic of Georgia write curricula. I recall Ashot, a teacher from Armenia, saying that they should have Christian dogma throughout their curriculum. The university professors cautioned Ashot about the concept of "separation of church and state." Ashot went on to claim that it would be alright in Armenia, where 99% of Armenians are Christian. Later, Ashot explained that although he did not believe in God, he was undoubtedly a Christian because everyone in Armenia was. Ashot plainly believed that he inherited his faith, rather than having to do or believe anything – not unlike a lot of "Christians" and others in America. I was thinking that believing in God, believing that Jesus Christ was His Son, and that Jesus died and was resurrected on the third day were **the** major tenets of Christianity. Thus, when asked if I am "religious" or a "Christian" I respond by saying that Jesus Christ is my Lord and Savior. Truly, the words "religion" and "Christian" mean different things to different people. Christianity is a relationship with Jesus Christ, not just going to Church and thinking that one is a good person – and certainly not simply being born into a believing household in a country that is mostly Christian.

In various surveys from the early 1990's, over 80% of Americans claimed to be Christians. More recent surveys place that number at about 76%. We have taken the Bible and prayer out of public schools and the United States is suffering the repercussions of that. I was listening to *Primerica* on my car stereo about a year ago. The topic was the infamous word "tithing." *Primerica* claimed that statistics show that only about 4% of Americans truly tithe – i.e. give 10% of their gross salary to the local church that they attend. When I think about what it really means to be a Christian, I think that "4%" may be closer to the amount of true Christians in this country, rather than the roughly 80% who claim to be.

My parents named me "Troy," which means warrior, because they thought that was a neat name and meaning for me to be associated with. In a way, this book addresses the battles that I have experienced – physically, emotionally, and spiritually. This is the story of my personal spiritual growth, and my hope is that this story will help you grow, too. My intention with this book is not to "judge" others, but to simply address scriptural truths that I have experienced in my life.

Troy

Chapter 1
In the Beginning...

"How can you love God?" "You used to wrestle, coach and be a weight lifter. I wanna know how you can now sit there in that wheelchair and be so upbeat?"

I have heard questions like these a lot in the past few years, and my answer is simple and requires very little thought. I usually reply, "Jesus is the reason! People around me are typically the negative ones that tend to bring me down. Jesus is the only one who continually gives me peace and joy." Occasionally, my response will lead to deeper discussions and great witnessing opportunities, which is why I welcome such questions. I can easily relate my current situation to David's in Psalm 6:6-10, which reads:

> ⁶ I am worn out from groaning;
> all night long I flood my bed with weeping
> and drench my couch with tears.

⁷ My eyes grow weak with sorrow;
they fail because of all my foes.

⁸ Away from me, all you who do evil,
for the Lord has heard my weeping.

⁹ The Lord has heard my cry for mercy;
the Lord accepts my prayer.

¹⁰ All my enemies will be ashamed and destroyed;
they will turn back in sudden disgrace.

I also cannot help but think of Job and how he was treated by his friends and loved ones because of the trials that he was allowed to experience from Satan. Job's own wife told him to curse God and die! Job began to question God in chapters 38-42. And then God reminded Job that He was the Creator of all things, the Alpha and the Omega, the Beginning and the End, and that Job had no reason to question His will. Job stayed faithful to God through these trials, repented from his questioning of God, and was blessed unimaginably during the latter part of his life because of it.

I am in no way comparing the trials that I have faced in my life to Job's, but seeing what Job went through, and being aware of my own occasionally ungodly behavior, I cannot help but think of the blessed life that I have despite the trials that I continue to face.

"Troykie"

I had a few nicknames growing up, as I imagine most children do. There were the more unpleasant names that Dad used to call me at a pretty young age – things like "Maggot" and "Goober," both of which he meant jokingly. Since I had no idea what those terms actually meant, they didn't really bother me. Of course, as I grew to understand the unpleasant meaning of those terms, joke or not, I no longer cared for those nicknames. I could never figure out why any man would choose to call his child by these nicknames.

Once in awhile Dad would refer to me as "Troykie." This was a much nicer and loving nickname, one that I preferred. It symbolized innocence and youth. This is the only nickname Mom ever called me. At the age of three, my family lived in Grimes, Iowa, a northwest suburb of Des Moines. Dad worked for Iowa Public Television at the time, and we had already moved once during my life from another Des Moines suburb. I do not remember living in my place of birth at all. Even though neither of my folks were in the military – and thus *required* to frequently relocate – we usually lived in a different location every two to four years. This was generally not to most of my family's liking, but Dad was old school: If he said something, then that was the way it would happen, without question. I really don't know why we moved so often. Perhaps Dad thought that he would find happiness and a new life with each new place. I am not sure. Occasionally we actually did move for Dad's work, but that was the exception, not the rule.

My first childhood memory started off pleasantly, but did not end up quite so pleasant. I was alone in a wading pool in my backyard, enjoying a sunny, summer day. A beautiful black and gold thing flew up to me. It made a neat buzzing noise. I reached out to hold it... It stung me with a pain that I had never known! That was how I was introduced to bumble bees. I did not like it, and I could not figure out why the beautiful, buzzing thing did something so mean. I started wailing. Mom rushed out to snatch me up and apply proper medical procedures. Mom was wonderful. She always knew what to do or how to make things right. Many years later, as I began to understand more about our heavenly Father and how He tends to His children, I would recognize how the way that Mom would tend to me was not unlike the way that God mercifully tends to our needs and comforts us in our times of trouble.

My brother, Shane, is also pretty wonderful. He is four and a half years older than I, and often served as my guardian. We had our normal sibling rivalry, but when he wasn't picking on me, he always watched out for and protected me. If anybody else messed with me, they would have to answer to Shane. That is how it should be with brothers.

One night, in that same year as the bumble bee, I was terrified because of a bad storm. Shane let me sleep in his bedroom on his trundle bed. He comforted me by singing:

"All night, all day,
angels watching over me, my Lord.
All night, all day,
angels watching over me."

I am a creature of obsessive habit. I always have to make sure light switches are in the down position, I always have to end my last step when going up or down stairs on my right foot. I have sung that once comforting and now annoying song every single night after bedtime prayers for the past 34 years. I will not sleep peacefully if I do not. I sing it silently, in my head, of course. I would not want anyone to think that I was crazy.

The first birthday party that I remember with any detail was for my fourth birthday. Mom always made the coolest cakes and threw the greatest parties. Mom was MacGyver, I am sure of that. It seems that everything these days must be purchased. But when I was growing up, I do not recall one Halloween costume or birthday party that was bought at a store, and yet they were always very cool. Mom always found time to read my favorite book to me...over and over and over again. She always wore down her body entertaining me, the active child. As long as it was appropriate, Mom would always play what I wanted to play, and she always came up with other creative games for us to play. The games we played, however, made me think, learn, were fun, and they did not cost a penny. These days, if it cannot be bought, most people do not want to hassle with creating it.

I began my life of mischief pretty early. I remember my friend and I mixed up a milk carton of mud and then dumped that on the neighbor kid's head, just because we thought it would be funny. As the young boy cried, my friend and I laughed. I did not think of the punishment that I would later receive from my parents for this act of cruelty. As children, we often do not consider the consequences of our cruelty – not for ourselves and certainly not for the victims of our mischief.

Mom and Dad gave me well-needed spankings on occasion. Today, it is often viewed as a horrendous act to spank your kids. I understand that abuse can stem from spanking, but if done properly out of love, not anger, spanking is a useful tool. I do not remember getting spanked more than a couple of times past a very young age. I honestly think that kids do not want to disappoint their parents by doing something wrong more than even the threat of spanking, so they do not do what they know may disappoint Mom and Dad. At least that has been my experience and it seems to me that a few appropriate spankings at an early age can be all that it may take to guide children down the right path to being more obedient.

> Train a child in the way he should go,
> and when he is old he will not turn from it.
> — Proverbs 22:6

> Do not withhold discipline from a child;
> if you punish him with the rod, he will not die.

> Punish him with the rod and save his soul
> from death.
> — Proverbs 23:13-14

Spanking can be done appropriately with wonderful results. I believe that I am living proof, even if I do say so myself.

When I was four years old, Dad decided he wanted to be known as a "farmer." He bought a tractor and drove it around town. We moved 90 minutes south of Des Moines to a 40-acre farm. Dad still worked at Iowa Public Television, so I am not sure why we moved. On the farm, my tendency to be accident-prone began to render serious and negative results, and that was where my fear of snakes began.

In Grimes, I was very intrigued by garter snakes. My friend, Chris, and I used to catch garter snakes in the field across from his house – and that's when the mischief would begin. (I do **not** recommend that anybody do this or any of the foolish things I describe in this book.) Chris and I would catch them and put them in a minnow bucket. When we had gathered several snakes, we would dip them in oil and throw them on the windshields of passing cars. At the time we thought this was hilarious. But if this happened to me today, I would have a serious accident due to my adult terror of snakes.

That love of snakes became fear with one terrifying event while living on the farm. On the neighboring acreage lived a hog farmer. He had a big gathering down by his pond one weekend, and my family was invited. At the time, I always wanted to be the center of attention. So, being in front of dozens of people, I wanted to show the crowd my "muscles" by rolling over an old abandoned motor from some sort of machine. Lo and behold, upon rolling the motor over, there was a huge bull snake, a "monster" that was longer than I was tall. It frightened me beyond anything words can explain. I was rescued when one of the other farmers disposed of the snake and Mom did her motherly thing to comfort me. I have been terrified of snakes ever since that moment. I think the unsuspected presence of snakes is what terrifies me most.

Certainly this huge bull snake was nothing like the little garter snakes that I was familiar with.

My first real accident happened when my brother Shane and I went hiking in the woods a few miles away from home when I was around five years old. There was a ravine about eight to ten feet deep. A tree had fallen, making a perfect bridge crossing the ravine. I, of course, decided I needed to cross this ravine. (I suppose it was more of a ditch than a ravine.) Crossing a log in old cowboy boots was probably not a terribly good idea. I slipped and fell off of the tree into the ditch, and I cracked my head on a rock at the bottom of the ditch. Now my brother had to somehow calmly walk me back to the house more than a mile. When we made it home, Mom did her "thing." I was always amazed how Mom could be a chef, a teacher, and a doctor, but she seemed to be just that. I was bleeding profusely, but Mom decided that I would not need stitches, so she did what she could to mend me. It was not pretty, but it worked.

My second accident *did* require stitches. Shane and I were sledding one winter in another ditch not far from our front yard. I got going pretty good once and could not stop myself or bail out before I tangled with a fallen tree. The tops of the tree's branches were facing me. I eventually was stopped when the branches went into my throat. Luckily, we did not have as far to walk home. This time, Mom decided this was beyond her medical abilities and that the wound would require stitches. She rushed me to the hospital where I received nine stitches. The doctor said that the branches had scratched the bottom of my tongue and that I was lucky: the branch had missed my larynx by about a centimeter. I did not yet know then who God was, but clearly I had been blessed by the work of His hand my whole young life so far.

I started kindergarten on the farm in Osceola, Iowa, but did not finish there. The frequent moving continued. This, however, was the only time it was for a job. I am not sure why Dad left Iowa Public Television. He seemed to love it and the people who worked with him there. He was a graphic artist and I loved visiting him at work there. I got to see the neat backdrops and other projects he created. Iowa Public Television was the home of many kids shows, so it was very fun to see all that went into creating those shows.

I am not really sure of the reason for our next move, but Dad probably saw it as a financial opportunity, and so the Langos family headed for brand new territory in Anoka, Minnesota. Anoka is near Minneapolis, where I was introduced to gophers – and to mosquito bites as I had *never* known.

It is here that I also learned to ride a bike and had my first crush. To learn how to ride a bike, Dad started me at the top of a grassy hill and pushed me down the hill on the bike. Dad did things that way because that was the way that they were done to him, and that is what he knew. You must realize that this is a man who learned how to swim when his own Dad threw him off of a dock into a lake and said "I'll see you back at the house."

My first crush was on the neighbor girl, Candy. She also planted my first kiss on the lips. Minnesota also got me started on the path of true debauchery. Believe it or not, I saw my first R-rated film when I was just in kindergarten. I also had my first taste of wine. These were both sort of by accident, but when I was older, I certainly remembered them.

There were some memorable events, however, that happened up north in the Minnesota area in our brief six months there. I remember the Shakopee natural habitat zoo, where I saw my first and only beluga whale. Of course, Valley Fair would be memorable to any child. There I recall "The Floom" log ride, and I also remember petting a Boa Constrictor. Yes, a big ol' snake. They were not actually as frightening when being held by a trainer and, though it was probably about 12 feet long, it was always in my sight with no slithering surprises. And how could I forget the Apple River in Western Wisconsin? As a child I remember falling out of my inner tube on the rapids. Bystanders yelled "Save the child, save the child!"

as Dad grabbed me by the hair, perhaps saving my life in the wild rapids.

The Langos family moved again after only six months. Dad's reason for moving to Minnesota had been for a job. At the time he worked for a well-known evangelist, and he quit after six months due to a terrible experience with this evangelist. When Dad left, the evangelist said to Dad that if he ever said anything bad about him, he would sue. About the only thing I will say about this situation is that it was not helpful for Dad's spiritual relationship with God. We moved then to Altoona, Iowa, part-way through my first grade year. Altoona was the longest we ever stayed in one house: over eight years.

My career at Altoona Elementary did not begin very promising. I got onto the wrong bus and ended up at the wrong school on my first day. When I finally got to the correct school, I was placed in a reading class that was apparently more than I was capable of handling. This was way too much for a new first-grader to handle all at once. I ended up crying, which got me labeled as a "baby." Kids are harsh, aren't they? After I was in an environment that I felt comfortable with, things seemed to be alright.

I actually became a good student. In elementary school I eventually got involved in Talented and Gifted programs, I learned to write my own computer programs, I won the 3rd grade spelling bee and the all-school spelling bee in 4th grade. I won the school-wide fire prevention poster contest. My poster had an ignited match drawn on it next to a burned forest. The caption read: "You would never think something so small could cause something so big." (Today that kind of reminds me of James 3:5: **"Likewise the tongue is a small part of the body, but it makes great boasts. Consider what a great forest is set on fire by a small spark."**) Academic success continued for the rest of my life through graduate school.

In the spring of my first grade year, Mom and Dad told me that I must play a sport – for socialization more than anything. So in the spring of 1979, I went out for Little League baseball. Clearly, baseball was not my sport. After that, I did not want to do sports anymore, but my folks made me try soccer and if I did not like that, I would not have to play sports anymore. During the fall of second grade I went out for soccer. I was pretty fast and coordinated, and so soccer seemed to fit me like a glove. I ended up playing soccer for fourteen years and coaching it for five years during the years I was teaching. Thank goodness my folks made me play a sport.

The Nominal Christian

By second grade, I had already been exposed to alcohol and inappropriate movies. But I knew kids that were already engaged in drugs, drinking, and smoking. I may have gotten involved with these things if not for my Mom making a huge sacrifice that I am ever so grateful for. When I was in second grade, Mom went back to work, leaving my brother and me as latch-key children, with no supervision in the mornings before school, nor in afternoons before she got home. I started to get into all sorts of trouble at school. The "good kid" that everybody knew was even getting disciplined at school and having my teachers call for meetings with my parents. Why? To get attention again? I do not know for sure, but that is probably a pretty safe guess. Mom quit her job and became a baby-sitting housewife. Before laws limited how many kids a person could watch in a "day-care" at one time, Mom would baby-sit twelve kids at once. She did a great job with that, all for the sake of being home for me before and after school. It must have worked. I never got into trouble at school again and my "good kid" reputation began to ring true. My greatest "no-no" was the "potty mouth" I seemed to have as a child.

One thing I am most grateful to my parents for is that they introduced me to Jesus Christ. At the age of nine, with Mom and Dad watching over me, I knelt by the side of my bed and prayed the Sinner's Prayer and accepted Jesus Christ as my Savior. I was serious, and it was then that I *really* began my life as a "good kid." I am not sure that I completely understood what a relationship with Christ was or how it could impact my life. Back then I saw it as a "get out of jail free card" and I did not grasp the "Lordship" idea yet. In all sincerity, I do believe I received salvation at that moment. Romans 10:9 says: **"If you confess with your mouth, 'Jesus is Lord,' and believe in your heart that God raised him from the dead, you will be saved."** This does not say that you *might* be saved, but that you *will* be saved. So, today I do believe in things like deathbed repentance, but as a baby Christian I had some growing up to do.

I started going to church and doing Bible lessons with my family for a year or two at this point in my life. But both my relationship with Christ and my Dad's were pretty much just "going through the motions." Dad did not tithe. He claimed he was "giving his time." Apparently he thought that was enough. Certainly the Bible instructs us to make disciples and do good works, but it also instructs us to tithe, to not put our trust in money, but in God. Looking back now, I can see that I disagree with Dad's view on tithing and time, but at the time I wasn't really making any disciples myself. Witnessing was just too uncomfortable. So, Dad and I just kept going through the motions of our relationship with Christ.

Don't get me wrong. Dad did many great things. I specifically remember him paying off Grandma's house one Christmas. I remember her crying tears of happiness. Dad did many wonderful things for his family and all sorts of people, but after about fourth grade, I did not hear many praises to God from Dad, if any. I would later have to learn that salvation is not earned: **"For it is by grace you have been saved, through faith – and this not from yourselves, it is the gift of God – not by works, so that no one can boast."** (Ephesians 2:8-9).

My Dad

I should talk a bit about Dad's background at this point. Dad's mother gave him up for adoption. He was abused at an orphanage until he was six years old, when he was adopted by the woman that I knew as Grandma Langos. Dad was a Vietnam veteran, who only recently was diagnosed with Post Traumatic Stress Disorder (PTSD). That has not helped with any of his relationships, as one symptom of PTSD is an inability to have serious relationships or be around people for any length of time. One night in Vietnam, Dad was asked to take another soldier's patrol duty. Had he not done that, he would have been firebombed with the rest of his troop.

Mom was pregnant with my brother, Shane, when Dad was drafted and he did not think he would see his first boy or see his wife ever again. Shane was born when Dad was in Vietnam, so Dad did not know his first son for more than the first year of his life. I think this is the reason that Dad does not have a strong relationship with Shane and tends to "good cop-bad cop" both of the relationships with his sons today. I always hated the double standard Dad held for me and Shane.

My Dad was a bit racist after the war. One event in Vietnam really made that worse. One day a group of soldiers had been assigned to perimeter guard duty, and a small group of them who happened to be black took their weapons and holed up in the mess hall, refusing to go out there. The situation was eventually defused and the soldiers disciplined, but that certainly didn't help my Dad's attitudes toward black people. After the war, Dad worked in a couple of different situations that just fanned the flames. In both cases, black men came to work with my Dad and later were caught doing drugs on the job, and they just generally "flaked out" and did not show up for work. One of them even stole money from the place. Dad said the jobs they had were pretty good, and so he didn't understand why those men would throw their lives away like that. It certainly didn't help my Dad view black people any more favorably.

Times were sometimes tough for my Dad. Once, Dad had to lay off everyone from a company where he worked, including himself. With the unemployment running out and having had over a hundred job applications turned down, Dad saw no relief in sight. When I came home from school one day, Dad told me that he had tried to kill himself that day and even failed at that. With tear-stained eyes Dad told me this story, and that he had accepted a $6 an hour job in a factory because nobody would hire a 40-plus-year-old white man with no college degree. That day probably drew me closer to Dad than anything ever has. It was not in his nature to cry, certainly not in front of his son, but he did cry while embracing me.

A Turning Point

In seventh grade, at the urging of some friends, I reluctantly began to wrestle competitively. At first I did not really like wrestling. I thought it was just rolling around with a bunch of sweaty guys. Of course, I had only known the acting that I saw in All-Star Wrestling on television, not actual wrestling. Football was actually my greatest love. I used to play backyard football all of the time, and my speed made everybody want to be on my team, which I also loved. I always loved being the center of attention; in class, at family functions, and in sports. But I was a small fry and there aren't too many 80-pound tailbacks in college or the NFL. (That's what I weighed in seventh grade) So I thought I would give this wrestling thing a try. I remember taking down an eighth-grader who was on the first team in a mini take-down tournament that was held during my first practice. Thanks to the adoration and surprise I received from coaches and fellow wrestlers, I was hooked! Wrestling would write a new chapter in the story of my life and in this book.

Chapter 2

The Rebellious Jock

I ended up having a pretty decent wrestling career in junior high school. I had a winning record, made it to the finals of some tournaments, and I started to become recognized for my wrestling ability at school. I went on to experience a great high school career, the highlight of which was when I made it to the state semi-finals against an opponent I truly believed that I would beat. Thirty seconds into the match, however, I received a foot sweep that cracked some bones and snapped some ligaments in my ankle, thus ending my season and dashing my hopes. But this happened my junior year, so I had the hope of a promising senior year to obtain my ultimate goal of becoming a state champion.

However, my focus got a bit sidetracked my senior year by a beautiful junior girl whom I had my eyes on for a couple of years. She was quite attractive, and her being fairly well-built did not chase me away by any means. After all, I was still a teenage boy. But I think what also attracted me to her was her "innocence." I did not want any distractions from achieving my goal of being a state champion, so I had vowed not to date during wrestling season. But this girl came from a nice, church-going family and seemed to be the kind of girl that I could date without violating my desire to not get involved with promiscuity.

My senior year I attained a #1 ranking in wrestling. In the state quarter-finals, however, I was defeated 7-4 by the wrestler that had been ranked #2. I never recovered and I never attained my ultimate goal of becoming a state champion wrestler. But at least I still had my raving beauty to comfort me. It was not the same thing, but it was still nice.

I ended up taking her to prom that year. We double dated to prom and went to my brother's house after dinner and the dance. Although my date did not know I heard her say this, the other couple had spent some "time" in my brother's bedroom. When the other couple was "finished" in my brother's bedroom, I heard my date ask the other girl if she had fun. My date then said, "I don't blame you. If I had a boyfriend, I'd be in there, too." I thought we had been dating for almost four months? What was I to her? I had thought she was not into that, which made things easier for me. My date was one of only two girls in high school that I had told that I loved. Since I would not have sex with either of them, I do not know if I was just trying to "trick" them into liking me or not, but at the time I don't think I even knew what those words truly meant. I didn't say "I love you" to anyone after high school until 10 years later, when I learned with my future wife what unconditional love truly is.

My Dad always kept a loaded .357 Magnum downstairs on the end table next to the recliner by the TV. That was not a smart thing to do, but he did it for protection. I do not know why he did that anymore than I know why we moved so often. One night shortly after prom, I was home alone. I put the barrel of that loaded gun into my mouth. I am not sure if I was just experimenting with the idea of "What would this be like?" or not. I probably was, but later I came to know how that would have affected others if I had pulled the trigger. Years later, a friend and former roommate of mine got "dumped" by his girlfriend, got drunk and took his own life with just such a gun. That was terrible and I never understood how the smartest guy that I knew – a guy that had made partner of the law firm that he worked for by the time that he was in his late twenties – could think so lowly of himself. How could he feel bad enough to take his own life when it seemed that he had so much going for him? It was probably the alcohol, but I will never know in this life. Thank goodness that I did not drink alcohol at this time in my life or the results may have been much different for me.

But at that time I thought "What's the point?" I refrained from drinking, partying, and promiscuity because I thought that God would reward me for being a "good boy" by granting me that ambition of becoming a state champion. Well, look what that got me; a stinking 6th place finish to go along with a broken ankle my junior year and a #1 ranking my senior year which turned out to be just ink on paper, no gold medal to show for it. I also had to hear those painful words from a girl whom I thought I was honoring and being a nice boy with.

After the state wrestling tournament my senior year, I did an abrupt about-face. Instead of realizing that maybe I just was not as good as I thought I was, I blamed God for my broken ankle my junior year and my defeat my senior year. I had thought I could earn brownie points with God and that I deserved a state championship if I was a "good kid." Jesus was my Savior at this time in my life, but it was clear that He was *not* my Lord. So from that point on I let the world dictate my behavior, and I rebelled against God, my parents, and my disciplined training. I began a life involving women and wine – quickly realizing that when I was drunk on wine, it was much easier to get with women. There weren't many weekends after high school without either wine or women as my new goal for attaining happiness.

Before I left for college, I remember slow dancing with Mom in my bedroom to the song "God Only Knows" by the Beach Boys. In a sense, that was an emotional moment of saying "goodbye." The Beach Boys were my favorite childhood band, so that moment with Mom also signified that her baby boy had grown up. Mom and Dad made the four-hour trek to college with me to drop me off. I remember Mom saying that Dad had his own emotional moment and cried the entire four-hour trip back home. I had only seen Dad cry that one time I mentioned earlier, but now he must have been thinking about little "Troykie" being all grown up.

After the state wrestling tournament my senior year, I had no intention of wrestling again. I was planning on going to the University of Northern Iowa, which was known for its great education program. I knew I wanted to teach, so this seemed like the school I should attend. Al Baxter, however, was the wrestling coach at Buena Vista College and somehow talked me into wrestling for him. Though I was reluctant, I ended up wrestling for the "Big Beaver." (A beaver was our mascot.) But I chose not to give up partying and had a very average collegiate wrestling career as a result. This "God thing" had not worked out for me, so why should I sacrifice living "the good life" for God or anyone else?

My junior year of high school at the state wrestling
tournament, 135 pound weight class (me on right).

My junior year in Buena Vista College, 150 pound weight class.

Another chapter in my life would begin in college, along with the popularity that came with it: singing. It all started with me trying to draw attention to myself again at a karaoke bar. The first karaoke tune I ever sang was "Yesterday" by the Beatles. After I sang it the first time, a girl came up to me and said that her sister was looking for somebody to sing at her wedding in a few weeks and was having no luck finding anybody. She wondered if I would do it. I was drunk, but I was flattered and said that I would. This ended up landing me singing in about twenty weddings over the next several years, and led to a group of gentlemen asking me if I would be the front man for their alternative rock band. I loved that idea, so I said Yes. We ended up being called Prisoners of Tradition, which spoke for the "rebels" against society that we thought we were.

During my junior and senior years of college, I ended up living in a college-owned house that was technically off campus, a place called Fracker Cottage. My junior year I lived with seven other pretty fun and nice guys. My girlfriend at the time thought that the guys at Fracker Cottage were all very nice. So I was pretty enraged when she said that at freshman orientation, the Resident Advisor (RA) had told her something quite different. When I asked her what the RA had told this group of freshmen girls, she said, "The RA said that the guys at Fracker Cottage would coax girls into their bedrooms and then slam the doors shut, and have somebody else lock the door with the dead bolt that was on the outside of the doors, so that they could have their way with the girl." My response was, "WHAT! The RA actually told that to you girls? Clearly, we don't do that nor do we even have dead bolts on our doors." Fracker Cottage usually was occupied by jocks. My senior year I ended up living there with seven other men, most of them wrestlers. Now, I know college athletes usually get an unfair stereotype about being sexually aggressive, and sometimes it unfortunately is true. I think several of us in the house my senior year were pretty promiscuous. Eventually the rumor ended up dying down, but I did not take well to being called a rapist by anybody, least of all by another student who was employed by the college.

Prisoners of Tradition practiced in the house and held parties during some of our practices until we could do the same at a cheap, off-campus warehouse that was much bigger than our basement at Fracker Cottage. I must say, however, that the best (at least the most fun) "gigs" we ever had were at an end of the year yard party held in the backyard at Fracker Cottage (complete with "wet-banana" water sliding) and at a VIESHA fraternity party that had over 2,500 people in attendance. (VIESHA is the name of a week-long festival at Iowa State University.) Most of the crowds that we had played before were between 100-

500 people, so it was exciting to sing in front of a crowd that size. My need for attention was certainly satisfied at that party.

My undergrad days came to a close in May of 1994, and so did my role with the band. But I loved to sing and singing in the shower just wasn't "cutting" it. So I asked Dad if I could have his guitar, since I had not heard him play it for nearly a decade, and I taught myself how to play basic chords. After graduation I ended up being hired to teach social studies and serve as the assistant varsity wrestling coach at a notable high school. That would suffice for the time being, as I could attend graduate school during nights and summers while achieving my PhD and going on to teach college, which was what I thought I wanted.

As an assistant wrestling coach I worked with a varsity coach whom I grew to respect and admire as a dear friend. We lovingly called him "Redhead." He wrestled at the University of Iowa under Dan Gable. Redhead taught me practical techniques that I had never known. I became twice the wrestler as a coach than I ever had been as an athlete.

The Jock Becomes a Singer?

The prospect of a singing career also started to become interesting at this time. After Prisoners of Tradition broke up and I taught myself how to play guitar, I started writing my own music. I continued singing and playing guitar at weddings and karaoke bars. My traditional favorite karaoke tunes were "Mandy" by Barry Manilow (I can thank Mom for that) and "I Cross My Heart" by George Strait. I even sang that one at a wedding once and it got me into the finals of a contest. After the semi-final round of that contest, one of the judges told me to pick a more upbeat tune and have a more lively routine. I should have stuck with what I was good at. But NOOO! The entertainer that loved attention would have his stage. At that time, the television show "Ally McBeal" had a dancing cartoon baby that danced to the song "Hooked on a Feeling." I thought this would be perfect. So I practiced "Hooked on a Feeling," made a baby bonnet, and borrowed a cloth diaper from the mother of a friend who lived in town. It was time for the finals of the contest and a chance to win $1000. I walked out on the stage to laughter. I could not help but notice right in the front row was Tim Dwight, an Iowa Hawkeye legend who went on to play in the NFL. The song started, but it was a slow version, not the "Ooga Chaka, Ooga Chaka" version that I had intended and rehearsed. I ran off of the stage to booing. This was not the attention I wanted to receive. I do not embarrass easily, but that time I really was embarrassed. I should have stuck with George Strait.

Apart from a couple of songs from Hank Williams, Jr., Alabama, Charlie Daniels, and Randy Travis, I don't even like country music – but I was always told I sang it well. (Once I got to sit on Charlie Daniel's bus and talk to him. I am so happy that he has come to know Christ.) The fact that people liked my country singing piqued my interest enough that I wrote to a real estate tycoon I know who lives in Des Moines and owns a recording studio in Nashville, Tennessee. He represents some pretty big names in the country music industry, so he sent a music track demo to a studio in Des Moines. I drove to Des Moines to lay down a voice track. I did get another job from this singing a commercial for Drake Diner in Des Moines. On the demo sent by the producer in Nashville, there was one track called "It Was Just Another Tuesday" that reminded me of a good friend and teaching colleague who had a brain aneurism and died in his shower. He was only in his early forties and left behind a wife and two children, one of whom I am told is the one who found him in the shower. He died on a Tuesday and the song made me think of his wife and kids and how horrible that must have been. Anyway, the tape with my vocals was sent to the producer in Nashville. The producer claimed that I had a great voice with lots of emotion, but that he would like me to move to Nashville, so that he could work with me. I was at a job that I loved and at which I was good, so I was in no hurry to move to a new city for country music, which I did not even like. So I kept teaching,

My alternative rock band in college had also sent a copy of a CD we had made to Rodell Records in Los Angeles. They thought we had a song with commercial potential and a couple of the guys in my band entertained the idea of moving to LA to "give it a shot." I had just gotten the teaching job that I would start in the fall, and I had my doubts anyway. We were a decent band, but I did not think we were "commercial potential" good. Then again, I would not call many of today's popular rock or country bands very musically talented, and yet they sell records.

So after the Nashville incident, I did think to myself that this is the second time I turned down a chance to potentially become a career musician. Producers are not going to fly to Iowa and bend over backwards for a long-shot like me, but I was comfortable where I was, doing what I was doing. Maybe God had other plans for me, but I had backslidden from God and had not had a serious "heart-to-heart" with him for several years. At that point I would not know what a God-sent conviction would have felt like unless it literally bit me on the rear end.

So, I continued to do a job that I had grown to love: teaching.

I remember during the spring of my first year of teaching (1995) a student named April asked me if I would like to go to her church. I had not been to church since high school, but thought I would give it a try. I knew that I needed to start attending a good Bible-based church again anyway. I just knew it was something I should try again. So I told April that I would be there that next Sunday. I was impressed with the pastor's sermon. I set up an appointment to meet with him, at which I asked him if he had accepted Christ as his savior. This caught him a bit by surprise, but I said "Ya never know anymore." He said that he had, and he went on to tell me about a background that was strikingly similar, if not worse, than my own. He was a "lady's man," a wrestler, and involved in some pretty harsh drugs before he came to know Christ or got involved in the ministry. I believed this was a man I could listen to and believe every Sunday, so I started attending Grace Community Church that day. But I still had a lot of growing up to do.

Another favorite student of mine was a freshman with a small frame, but he was a pretty good kicker on the football team. He was on the sophomore team as a freshman, which rarely happened. I remember him kicking a game-winning field goal against the cross-town rival. That became a running joke all year whenever he would do or say anything goofy, I would always comment, "You kick a game-winning field goal and you think you run the world?" He went on to win a state title in football, basketball, and soccer all in one year. He kicked for the Iowa Hawkeyes and won the Lou Groza award. He now is *much* larger and kicks in the NFL for the San Diego Chargers. We called him "Kato." I also helped coach his sister in soccer. She was very good, but did not have much exposure to the JV squad that I ended up coaching.

I started coaching girls soccer my third year of teaching. I had my reservations about coaching girls, thinking that they would be a bunch of "cry babies." Boy, was I wrong! The girls worked harder than many of my wrestlers, complained less, and really tried to make their coach proud of them. I brought my wrestler's mentality to soccer, including more strenuous workouts than they had ever been exposed to, and they always did them without complaints. I quickly grew to love coaching soccer as much as wrestling. In all of my years teaching and coaching, I loved all of my students and athletes. I cannot think of many that I could not wait to see graduate and be done with.

One man it was hard for me to say good-bye to was the Dean of Students at the high school and the head football coach at the school where I worked. Reese was his name. He took over a football program that had not been used to winning, and they ended up winning three state championships in four years. He was a prince of a guy to boot, and after his third state title he was asked to help coach at the University of Iowa. Reese talked about this with his family, but he just could not pass up that opportunity and did go to work at Iowa alongside Kirk Ferentz. I missed Reese's character around the building, but I am very happy for him in his advancement.

There was only one other man at my workplace I even remotely considered with as high regard as Reese, and that was Coach "Hollie." He was the track coach and gym teacher. "Hollie" was a father figure to me and comforted me, giving me a shoulder to cry on during some of the tough times that I had during my early teaching career. "Hollie" and Reese are the kind of men I truly adore.

Not Quite Done with Rebellion

I suppose now that you have been introduced to a few men I admire, you should probably be introduced to a couple of my friends that I have not yet mentioned. There are a few incidents I could mention here that would not be very flattering for the people involved, and so I will not mention them all. So the two friends and few happenings I'll mention now are mainly just to give you an understanding of what type of goofballs we were.

These were certainly not the only goofy things we ever did, nor even close to the most fun, but they are the only remotely appropriate things that I care to share. Even today, I am nearly in tears laughing every time I get together with these two or talk to them on the phone. You may not find these things funny at all, but I still chuckle about them years after they happened. These few things I will mention all involve Chad and/or Jeff.

The first thing I find more funny than most people probably do happened at a party at Chad's house. I was talking with somebody else and Jeff was clear across the room. I was getting ready to take a sip of my drink and Jeff looks over at me and says in that high-pitched, silly voice of that cartoon witch from Bugs Bunny "drink it, drink it, drink it." He then clicks his feet together and runs off. I thought I was going to wet myself laughing so hard.

The next goofy thing that I still remember was when Chad, Jeff, and I had lunch at Hy-Vee. Jeff and I got the same lunch and sat down at a table. Chad came over, looked at the fact that Jeff and I both had the same thing, and in a serious tone said, "I was gonna get that too, but I felt sorry for the spaghetti."

The last thing I will mention happened when Chad and I were driving back on the interstate from something we had been doing far away. I was driving and Chad was starting to doze off. We came to our off-ramp. I checked to make sure no cars were near. The coast was clear, so I slammed on the brakes and screamed at the top of my lungs. Chad immediately snapped up in fear, thinking we were going to get into an accident or something. My laughing signaled to him that we were going to be alright, and that I was a big jerk. Many of the other funny things we did are really not appropriate to mention. I truly was goofy and was still a rebellious jock.

Chapter 3
Jesus Becomes My Lord

I started to get back on track with God in 1997. I was teaching a World Religions class, and a guest speaker in that class made a comment that got me thinking that I needed to live a more Godly life. I tried to get speakers for each of the religions that I covered in class. I often had guest speakers for Judaism, Christianity, Islam, Hinduism, and Buddhism. The guest speaker on Christianity was the pastor at Grace Community Church that I mentioned earlier. Generally, speakers would just field questions from the students. I remember a student sarcastically asking the speaker on Christianity if he loved God enough to die for Him. The pastor's response was what seriously began my road to becoming an actual, not just a nominal Christian. The speaker responded, "Of course I would die for Him. But anyone can be a martyr. I love God enough to *live* for Him." Ouch! I said my prayers each day. I went to church.

But was I living for God? Absolutely not! I was living for getting drunk and having sex. That part of my life would really start to change at a Promise Keeper's Convention in Minneapolis that August.

At the time, I had another very good friend named Dave. I had recently been attending a Bible study at his house, and we were in a flag football league together. Dave was pretty good. He had played quarterback at Cedar Falls high school. It was Dave who asked me if I wanted to attend a Promise Keeper's convention in Minneapolis in August of 1997. After he explained to me what that was, I said that I would go with him and a few other men.

The weekend message of the conference was "How can you expect others to change unless you are willing to change yourself?" I had certain family members who were very, very close to me who had not spoken to each other in years. This message of change hit a sensitive nerve. I desperately longed for these loved ones to reconnect, to change their ways and set aside their pride. Yet I, myself, had been unwilling to wholeheartedly commit to this concept. So with tear-stained eyes, and in front of tens of thousands of men, I made the alter call and accepted Jesus Christ as Lord of my life.

I am not saying that this improved my salvation status. I had already accepted that tremendous gift when I received Jesus as my Savior at the age of nine. I am also not saying that responding to that altar call made me any more perfect in any way. I will never be perfect and, although my actions were distinctly changed by the decision made on that day, it took me about three years to completely give up the booze. However, my drinking binges became noticeably fewer and further apart. And my out-of-wedlock "relations" ceased immediately except for one last incident. One of the few times I got drunk over the next few years (at a "going away" party for a friend), I ended up going back to a girl's home with her. You would think I would have learned that there is something to that saying "sex, drugs, and rock-n-roll." They all seem to go hand in hand. Other than those few times, accepting Jesus as my Lord made a big difference in my life and my behavior.

Amazingly, two of my dear friends, Matt and Mark, who were on the "wild side" with me in college, came to know Jesus as their Lord pretty close to the same time that I did. Matt was my arch-enemy in high school. I had beaten him at the district wrestling tournament to go to state my junior year and prevented him from going to state that year. Matt and I ended up wrestling together in college, and then we became best of friends. We both loved to be the center of attention. I remember we first bonded when we were walking through the hallways of our dormitory singing Lee Greenwood's "Proud to Be an American" at the top of our lungs. We later ended up living together at Fracker Cottage one year. I was the best man at his wedding and he was one of two best men at mine. (I could not decide between him and Chad, so both of them stood up as my best men.) Now Matt is very involved in church and teaches Bible studies. I remember him saying that he wanted to use my CD that I had composed and released in 2000 for a study based on the scriptures that inspired each song. I am not sure if he ever did that, but it honored me that he would even think to do that.

I recall many goofy things that Mark and I also did. One day, to the annoyance of many, we decided to sing everything we said as if we were opera singers. Mark was famous for several things I still do or say on occasion. If he had food on the side of his mouth, he would tell a person sitting at his table that they had food on the side of their mouth and point right at the food on his mouth, showing the person the area of their mouth the food was on. If somebody claimed that they really had to go to the restroom, he would say "show me" and expect them to do something, anything in response. Mark's favorite was for people to do what he liked to call "the pee-pee dance." I will let you use your imagination as to what that might have been. I used that when students would ask if they could use the restroom. He also used to warn people to be careful not to take too big of a bite of whatever they were eating, and then *he* would take a huge bite and gag it up. These are the fun things to me that I still remember about those two, and I am so proud of the spiritual walk that they are both taking now.

After the Promise Keeper's event in 1997, I continued to teach and coach with a new outlook on life. I remember getting a letter from one of my former wrestlers who attended Arizona State University that was very touching and a bit surprising. In it, he told me of how he had to write a paper about the most influential person in his life, and I was the one he wrote his paper about! I always loved this young man, but I was surprised to know that I had this impact on him. He said that he had no self-esteem, was short, heavy for his size, and that I was the one who continually encouraged him and gave him hope during practice his freshman year. I just thought that was my job. That is why I love teaching and coaching. He became a varsity wrestler before he graduated. I was proud of him. I wonder if there are any other stories like that I never knew about? I only know of a few that I will share before this book is over.

In the summer of 1998, another former wrestler named Keith asked me if I wanted to go with him to his home state of Idaho for a week. Keith and I had later become good friends, and on that trip I met his friends and family.

We ended up white-water rafting down the South Fork of the Boise River. That was a blast and it fit right into both of our adventurous and intense personalities. Keith had won a state championship in boxing when he lived in Idaho, and he was a state champion wrestler for Redhead and me when we coached him. But white-water rafting did not even compare to the adrenaline rush we got from what ended up being the highlight of our trip. We decided to go cliff jumping off of an 80-foot cliff into a crater lake. At the bottom of the cliff there lay about 12 feet of rocks we had to clear. We looked down and considered this risk for literally 45 minutes. Finally, Keith thrust both fists into the air and shouted, "Give me fuel, give me fire, give me that which I desire!" and made the jump. Seeing that he had easily cleared the rocks, I immediately followed him. It seemed as though it had been about a four second free-fall, but what a natural rush it was. It was fantastic! I always thought that every trip or vacation needed a theme song. Clearly "Fuel" by Metallica became the theme song of this trip. A few years later, Keith gave me a different type of honor by asking me to play a song that I had written at his wedding.

Me (L) and Keith (R) after our leap off of the 80 foot cliff.

After I had coached with Redhead for four years, Redhead decided that he wanted to pursue an administration degree and serves as a high school principal today. We still maintain a decent friendship, even though distance has separated us a bit. When Redhead left, I got hired as the interim head wrestling coach. Being the head coach at a major high school was another dream of mine come true. I had not inherited a team filled with "studs," but we were loaded with solid wrestlers throughout most of the line-up. I believed that we would be a solid dual meet team, but would likely not have more than one or two potential place-winners at the state wrestling tournament in February. Sure enough, we finished the season at 17-3 in dual meets, which was the most dual meet wins in a season that high school had ever posted at that time. I also finished second in the conference Coach of the Year votes. My team had beaten the team of the man that was voted first ahead of me. He retired that year, so I think he received some votes to honor his career. That was okay with me. At the state tournament that year, we did only have three qualifiers. None of them placed. This was a crushing disappointment to everyone, including me.

During the course of the season, after a speech I gave to the wrestlers at a practice one night, I had one mother tell me that her son came home all pumped up that night and told her he thought that I should be a motivational speaker. I was also told that same thing after a speech I had given and a song that I performed at the local Hawkeye Area Youth for Christ banquet. I always like to hear nice comments like that, but I never thought much about being a motivational speaker.

After the state wrestling tournament, I went in to ask our athletic director about the status of next year's coaching situation. He said that I had an excellent season and that he saw no reason to open the job up for interviews. So during the spring of 1999, I began my off-season regimen of planning summer camps, weight-training programs, and setting up individual sessions between each athlete and myself.

Lo and behold, and surprising to me in light of what I was told by the athletic director, the position of head wrestling coach *was* advertised and the interview process began. After months of screening candidates, it was narrowed to four finalists, one of which was the defending coach of the year in a different class. This worried me. I was finally called into the athletic director's office, where I was told, "Troy, this is one of the hardest things I've ever had to say." As the athletic director put his arm around me in an attempt to ease the pain from the words he was about to utter from his lips, he continued, "You're like a son to me. You have really matured these past few years and that has been fun to watch."

The athletic director was making a reference to the fact that he had noticed that I had started wearing ties and dressing nicely. That had come from a faculty meeting when the principal announced that, even though there was no dress code, he considered things like blue jeans inappropriate and he wished faculty did not wear them. I started wearing ties and stopped wearing blue jeans because he said he did not like that. First Peter 2:13-17 says that we must submit to authorities. I understand that to also include employers, and I believe that respecting employers gives honor to God.

The athletic director went on to say to me, "You did a great job this year and I appreciate the passion with which you carried out this job. The discipline you instilled and the level the kids' program has achieved through your efforts have been tremendous. But we're going with Mark." These were the most difficult words ever spoken to me. They ripped my heart out and sent me into months of emotional agony and crying myself to sleep each night.

The man hired was not the defending coach of the year, but a friend of mine with whom I used to coach with and who, when I asked him, had made no mention of even applying for this job. Mark was the athletic director's son. I felt betrayed in this entire situation, which is what made it so painful. Though contacted by other schools about coaching positions, I was hesitant to leave a teaching job that I had grown to love. Mark went on to build a great team, winning several state titles and I think getting the team ranked as high as fourth in the country. I was actually very happy for him, not at all bitter, but it was time for me to make a decision about my future.

So the first thing I did when other coaching positions crossed my path was to fervently pray. For months I fervently prayed. By June of 1999, I had been consistently convicted about the decision that I finally made. I asked God what He wanted me to do and this is what He told me: "I want you to be a husband and a father."

This struck me as particularly interesting because I had not known my future wife, Karen, in even a dating capacity. I had met her a couple of years earlier at my church, but there were no real "sparks" between us – and we certainly did not have any children yet. I am reminded of a book by Josh Harris called *I Kissed Dating Goodbye*. In it he says "The right thing at the wrong time is still the wrong thing." These words would prove to be prophetic for Karen and me.

Karen and me before we got married.

So, when it came time to decide about my future, I set my pride aside and kept the teaching job that I loved so dearly. I did acquire my M.A. at the University of Iowa through summer and night school, but I no longer desired to be a college professor. I continued to do what I loved, but without coaching wrestling – which had actually required more of my time than teaching. I did, however, continue to coach girls' soccer for a couple more years.

Instead of coaching, I decided to become an official and work wrestling meets and tournaments now and then. I never really fell in love with officiating as I had coaching and teaching, and so I gave it up after a year. I decided then to get involved in weightlifting competitions. (You see, that competitive edge never left me.) At that time I weighed 170 pounds, but I could bench press 335 pounds. When I entered my first weightlifting competition, I won easily. That sort of surprised the "big boys" who could lift much more than I could. But they did not realize that pound-for-pound I was a pretty solid young man, and this particular contest determined order of place according to how much you could lift in relation to the percentage of your body weight. I finished 12% ahead of the second place finisher.

That was in October of 2000. By then, I had been dating and finally proposed to my future wife. Thank goodness she accepted! That is a unique story in itself.

At the end of 1999, I had decided to hold an alcohol-free millennial New Year's Eve party. I invited friends from surrounding churches to celebrate New Year's Eve.

About 50 people showed up in all. Most people left before midnight to visit another party and ring in the year 2000. A few stayed back, one of whom was Karen. We ended up talking until 5 a.m. It really is amazing, because if I were still coaching wrestling, I never would have had this party. Why? To deter drinking among my wrestlers, I would have held a 6 a.m. practice on New Year's Day. But I remember going to bed as the sun was rising that morning thinking, "Why in the world did this encounter not occur years ago when we first met?" In my mind, Karen passed the T-graph of pros and cons with flying colors. She had chosen to make Jesus the Lord of her life, she was cute, she was funny, and she was a great conversationalist. I did not know we would end up getting married, but I knew she was the type of woman that I wanted to someday marry.

I called Karen for a follow-up date the next day. The New Year's Day bowl games did not seem to be as important as talking with Karen. We began our courtship as a result of that evening, but that never would have occurred if I were still coaching wrestling. I had a glimpse of God's plan and it was sweet. After a very pleasant meeting with my parents in April of 2000, in which Karen, Mom, and Dad seemed to "hit it off," I decided that I was in love with Karen. I had previously decided that if anyone could put up with me for six months (I had never previously dated anybody for more than three or four months) I would ask her to marry me. At this stage of our lives we were both in our late twenties and, through our previous dating experiences, we could figure out if any given relationship had potential or not. In June of 2000 I made the decision, even though I was only about 80% sure she would agree to marry me. I drove to a town known for quality rings and reasonable prices, got a ring, and invited her to a "mystery dinner." I actually used a nice card that she had sent me months earlier which I had saved, and I mailed back to her, inviting her to the dinner at my house.

When she came to the door, I put a blindfold on her and played the song "I Will Be Here" by Stephen Curtis Chapman. When the song was over, I told her she could take the blindfold off. On a sheet of paper I had written "I love you." Then I turned the page over and written on the back was the question "Will you marry me?" with the ring displayed. I was proposing to the woman I had grown to love, a love that I had never known with any other woman before. Just about a year before that proposal, I had decided to give up and quit trying so hard to meet Miss Right and just revel in my singleness. But thank you, God, she said "Yes!" We decided our day of matrimony would occur over a year from then to test the assurance of this emotional decision and the commitment level of our purity. But I was on cloud nine, as they say. I actually had nothing planned for dinner, so we went to "The Vine" for their famous chicken wings, which we both loved.

Deuteronomy 24:5 continued to register with me in ways that perhaps is not what was intended by the scripture, but what I took from it was to quit coaching and focus my life, besides on God, on Karen. That scripture reads, *"If a man has recently married, he must not be sent to war or have any other duty laid on him. For one year he is to be free to stay at home and bring happiness to the wife he has married."* I am not saying that people should stop doing all things that they are engaged in when they get married, but that was the conviction that I had. So I quit coaching altogether and directed my attention solely to God and Karen.

Chapter 4
God's Grace is Sufficient for Me

My life changed in new ways on January 26th, 2001. I was on my way to see a friend north of Waterloo. I had roomed with him before, and I knew that he was an atheist. He was smart and funny, but I knew from past attempts that he would not look at any Bible scriptures or listen to anything about God. Nonetheless, I had given him the book *More Than a Carpenter* by Josh McDowell, hoping that he would take the time to read it. During my trip to see him, I planned on discussing the book with him. That meeting never happened.

During my drive, I hit a stretch of black ice on the interstate, spinning me around and leaving my car at the side of the road. An SUV followed suit and rear-ended my Geo Tracker at 65 mph. It sent me skidding 40 yards down the shoulder. I do not remember any of it. The first thing I recollect was the paramedic asking me for my name and if I knew where I was. I apparently had broken my jaw, messed up my knee and shoulder, and with multiple cuts on my face that required 50 stitches. I also had a piece of windshield imbedded into my forehead. I remember the first time I saw myself in the mirror after all of my surgeries. I thought, "Oh no! I'm hideous!"

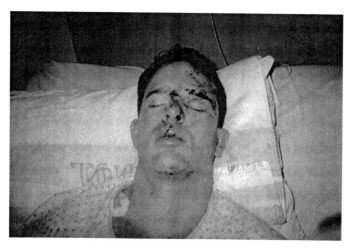

After my accident.

Besides a broken jaw, I had to have surgery on my shoulder and knee. The piece of windshield in my forehead gave me a splitting headache for about three weeks, but doctors said that it would eventually work itself out. One day it just popped out onto a table at which I was sitting. After all of the surgeries I had initially, the most painful surgery I had seemed minor in comparison. I temporarily had an arch brace in my jaw so that it would heal better where it was broken. My tongue kept brushing against the brace, creating what the oral surgeon called a granuloma. Imagine having a needle shot into your tongue and incisions and stitches put into your tongue to remove this granuloma. Then imagine finding out that this had to be done *again* when the oral surgeon realized that he did not cut deep enough, missing some of whatever this was. I have a remarkably high pain tolerance, but this tongue surgery was the worst pain that I had ever experienced.

The friend that I had intended to see was an attorney, and he agreed to handle my legal matters involving this accident case. He told me that I would be able to receive much more money than I was asking for. My response was that this was an accident, not malicious intent. If it were the result of irresponsibility, perhaps my attitude would have been more along the lines of what my attorney friend wanted. After all, if I would have arrived at the patch of black ice five minutes later, instead of getting rear-ended by that guy in the SUV, it would have been *me* hitting *him*.

My friend replied, "If you had hit him, he would sue you for more."

I said, "Maybe so, but I need to do what I think is right in the situation that did happen. I cannot think about what others would have done."

I opted to ask for the maximum amount that this man's insurance policy covered, not to sue him personally. The insurance maximum would cover my medical bills and a new car. That made me happy. To my attorney friend's dismay, that was the right thing to do.

I spent four days in the hospital initially after my accident. As I was instructed by doctors, I rubbed Vitamin E oil on my scars three times a day for several minutes. Within several weeks my scars aesthetically healed. By the grace of God, there just happened to be a plastic surgeon in the hospital the night of my accident. He had stitched me up nicely.

While in the hospital I experienced a moment I will never forget. It was late one night and I talked to God one on one. "God," I said, "I have led a great life and apart from marrying Karen, I have done everything I really want to do in life. I just wanted to say thanks for letting me live, but I was ready to go be with you if that was your will." Then I heard this voice in my head as clear as day. "I'm not done with you yet." That was it. I had no idea what was in store for me next.

The next few weeks at home gave me time to pray alone, cry alone, and memorize passages from scripture. I committed nearly 80 Scripture passages to memory during those few weeks, because I realized that I needed to take the time to do it. Adding several passages per year since,

I have now memorized over a hundred scriptures, but I am still shooting for the level that people like evangelist Jack Van Impe have attained.

In time, as I said, my scars began to heal. However, I began to experience blindness, fatigue, and restlessness. Doctors could not figure out what was wrong with me, but a neurologist at the University of Iowa had a suspicion. An MRI and a spinal tap confirmed in her mind that I had Multiple Sclerosis. So that is the disease I began to treat. Having heard about my diagnosis, my folks called while I was still in the hospital getting my initial treatments. One thing I will always remember Dad saying over the phone is "How can you love God?" My reaction was simple: "Who better to stand with?" (Romans 8:31 comes to mind: **"What, then, shall we say in response to this? If God is for us, who can be against us?"**) I was doing fairly well with this diagnosis. It was people around me – even *doctors* – bringing me down and depressing me.

One of the few encouraging comments came to me from my old coaching friend Reese, who had been coaching at Iowa for two years now. He made a pleasantly surprising visit to see me while I was still in the hospital. I had not seen him since he took the coaching job at Iowa. I will never forget his comment, and it's not surprising how he was able to bring the best out of his athletes. Reese told me, "The only thing you can control is your attitude."

He was right, and I try not to forget that, ever. That would have been a great response to my attorney friend's comment to me about suing for more money than I did. I love Reese and I sure miss being around him every day.

I discussed with Karen what we could expect with this disease and gave her a free pass to escape our engagement, guilt free. I am thrilled to report that she replied, "No way! Though we haven't exchanged vows yet, this engagement comes with the understanding that I am with you for better or for worse, for richer or for poorer, and until death do us part." God bless that wonderful woman! We got married on a beach in Mexico, underneath a rainbow at sunset on July 5th, 2001. No matter how hard I might have tried, I could not have scripted a more beautiful wedding story than that.

Chapter 5

The Music Man

During my "sick leave," apart from memorizing Scripture, I also had time to put words and music to some ideas I had, some of them for years. I've already mentioned my role as the front man in my college band (Prisoners of Tradition), whose music did everything *except* glorify God. When I changed paths after college, I learned how to play guitar and began composing contemporary Christian rock music. I am not a big hymn kind of guy, and I started to realize that there were some pretty great Christian bands out there – such as Third Day, Mercy Me, and Casting Crowns. Since I discovered bands like those, I very rarely listen to secular music anymore. In 2000, with friends helping on drums, piano, bass, and violin, I released a contemporary Christian rock CD, taking only good will offerings. Most of the guys and gals that helped me out all had families, but we were able to play a few concerts on request at a couple local churches, and a concert in the local pedestrian mall. After my accident, this time off finally gave me time to fine tune some of this new music.

Getting married in July of 2001 at first made things financially tight for Karen and me. We didn't know if we should put up the money to release another independent CD or not. We certainly did not think that we could afford to put the thousands of dollars that it would cost into another CD. So we prayed and we prayed and we prayed. Our conviction was not only to produce the CD, but to not even suggest a good will offering. We ended up selling a few at the local Christian book store. Overall we produced a thousand CDs with the new songs on them. Apart from the 82 that we sold at the local Lemstone Christian book store, we gave away the rest of the thousand CDs as a way to show the practical love of Christ.

I also sent a CD to the people in charge of distributing music at a local record store that is part of a national chain, FYE (For Your Entertainment). I was honored that the headquarters of that store sent me a letter back telling me that they were interested in carrying my record at 77 of their stores nationwide. I thought to myself, wow! But they had a lot of requirements that would basically make this a full-time job. If I had been 22-years-old again and not married, that would have sounded very appealing, but I loved my job and just really wanted FYE to sell the CDs. I do not think that they understood that is all that I wanted them to do. I was not about to drop thousands of dollars and tour at this juncture in my life for an uncertainty. So I told FYE that I would not be able to do everything that they required of me in order for them to sell my CD. That would have been very cool!

Another story that fits in nicely here is a story about Michael, a previous student of mine. Michael, as I remember, seemed a bit in opposition to societal standards. He was a friend of a boy who died from a drug overdose. In wrestling, I had coached the brother of the boy who died and I knew their family quite well. I gave the family a CD for comfort because I did not know what else to do. The family ended up playing a song off of the CD at the funeral. Months later I had a friend call me up and ask me if I knew Michael. I responded that I did, that he was a previous student of mine, and that I remembered his somewhat rebellious character. Apparently she knew Michael from a class that they had together at a Bible college. I pointed out that she must have the wrong kid. She then told me the whole story about his past, the drug overdose of his friend, and how one of my songs was played at the funeral. She told me how he ended up borrowing or purchasing a CD, and how he accepted

Christ as his savior as a result of the message on the CD. Wow! I have personally told dozens of people about Jesus, but that is the only person I know of who, by the work of God, had accepted Christ through anything that I could contribute. I hope there are many more out there that I do not yet know about.

Despite producing the CD on our own as newlyweds, before too long our financial hardships were amazingly resolved. Since those tough times, we have witnessed blessings that came from friends, family, loved ones, and we experienced some mysteries that Karen and I still cannot explain. We are not millionaires and probably never will be, but I do not at all worry about where my next meal will come from nor how we will pay our next energy bill. It is awesome! **God** is awesome.

I ended up taking a spiritual gift quest survey at my church to see what were my gifts and where my help would be most beneficial. When the results came in, the survey indicated that my number one gift was administration (and yet I have no desire to be a school administrator). Number two was teaching, which made me think that I was in the right occupation. Number three was no surprise to me: creativity (like writing music and poetry, I suppose). The thing that ranked dead last was not really a surprise, either, but was hard to see on paper in black and white: mercy. The leaders of that church then put me to work according to my spiritual gifts. I had already been leading the praise team musically, but my administrative talent was put to use when the church leaders asked me to put together a bi-annual worship schedule, so that singers and musicians would know who was scheduled to sing and when. I sort of enjoyed that. I became the contact person for the needs of praise team members. I did not mind that, particularly since nobody ever really called me. The leaders also had me teach a few lessons in the youth group. I enjoyed that, too. The thing I probably enjoyed most was when the church leaders asked me if I would lead and administer the youth group praise band. I got to choose whatever songs I wanted, and they were a bit more "rockin' " than what we played on the congregational praise ream.

One part of my personality became a common thread with all of these duties. That is, I am what some might call "anal retentive." I knew I was like this and dealt with this with my students at school. I am "old school." If I say to do something, just *do* it. If you have a conflict, do not tell me at the last minute unless it is an emergency. I do not do well with excuses and "whining." The spiritual gift quest survey had been right on: I *did* lack mercy. I am so glad that God has the mercy with *me* that I do not have with others.

My first contemporary CD had been titled "Goose."

That is the nickname that everybody used to call me in college, even some professors. At the time, I had wanted to make the CD a statement to my college comrades about how Jesus impacted my life. That's is why I chose to name the CD "Goose." But when I remixed that CD and put some new songs on it, the man that produced the new CD convinced me that "Goose" may have been a cute college nickname, but that this time I should simply call it "Troy Langos." So I did.

Chapter 6

Troy Langos: the CD

Track 1--Here I Am

Ephesians 6:18-20

> [18] And pray in the spirit on all occasions with all kinds of prayers. With this in mind, be alert and always keep on praying for all the saints.
>
> [19] Pray also for me, that whenever I open my mouth, words may be given me so that I will fearlessly make known the mystery of the gospel, [20] for which I am an ambassador in chains. Pray that I may declare it fearlessly, as I should.

"Here I Am" was the song played at the funeral of Michael's friend who had overdosed on drugs, the song that had led Michael to Christ. That phrase "here I am" appears many times in the Bible, but I think Ephesians

6:18-20 captures what I really wanted the song to convey. All of the songs I have ever written were intended to witness to other people, but this one ended up being a witness to me. I wrote this song in 1999, but this song took on a new significance for me when, in the hospital room after my car accident, God told me that He was not done with me yet.

Track 2—Gethsemane

Matthew 26-28, Mark 14-16, Luke 22-24

Rather than writing out three chapters from the Bible three different times, I will just comment that these are all the chapters describing events from the Last Supper to the Resurrection, including the night in the garden of Gethsemane before Jesus was crucified on the cross. I wrote this song shortly after 9/11/2001. I grew so tired of hearing people say "How can God let bad things happen to good people?" The real question is actually "How can God let *good* things happen to *bad* people?" Romans 3:23 tells us that nobody is good, so God's sacrifice of His son is merciful beyond what we deserve. We will never know the pain and suffering Jesus went through during the Passion Week. I hope we never do and I frequently thank God that He allowed His son to endure what He did for humanity's sake.

Track 3—Born Again

<u>Romans 7:21-25</u>

²¹ So I find this law at work: When I want to do good, evil is right there with me. ²² For in my inner being I delight in God's law; ²³ but I see another law at work in the members of my body, waging war against the law of my mind and making me a prisoner of the law of sin at work within my members. ²⁴ What a wretched man I am! Who will rescue me from this body of death? ²⁵ Thanks be to God—through Jesus Christ our Lord!

So then, I myself in my mind am a slave to God's law, but in the sinful nature a slave to the law of sin.

<u>Psalm 119:9-16</u>

⁹ How can a young man keep his way pure? By living according to your word.

¹⁰ I seek you with all my heart; do not let me stray from your commands.

¹¹ I have hidden your word in my heart that I might not sin against you.

¹² Praise be to you, O Lord; teach me your decrees.

¹³ With my lips I recount all the laws that come from your mouth.

¹⁴ I rejoice in following your statutes as one rejoices in great riches.

¹⁵ I meditate on your precepts and consider your ways.

¹⁶ I delight in your decrees; I will not neglect your word.

I had always wanted to write a song inspired by the longest chapter in the Bible, Psalm 119. I particularly wanted to focus on verses nine and ten. I also love Romans chapter 7, when Paul comments on the fact that he often does the things he does not want to do, but that the things that he wants to do, he does not do. This scripture seems like it was directed toward me, particularly in my more rebellious years. Psalm 119 and Romans 7 seemed to both fit into the type of song I wanted to write. "Born Again" also gave me a title track for the CD.

Track 4—Billy

"Billy" was not inspired by any particular scripture. It was inspired by my students and children in general. Children, in their innocence and simplicity, often seem to say such profound things unintentionally. "Billy" is not an actual person, rather a composite of children overall. My friend Dave, with whom I went to the Promise Keeper's convention in Minneapolis, ended up going to seminary in Grand Rapids, Michigan. After this CD was made, Dave told me a story about a nine-year old boy in a wheelchair named Billy that he had met when visiting a hospital in Grand Rapids. I had already written and recorded this song by the time that Dave met this boy. Dave gave the boy my CD to listen to. Hopefully it was a blessing to him. Again, without intention, this is another track on the CD that ended up being a powerful witness and good reminder to me. You will understand why later in this book.

Track 5—All I Need

2 Corinthians 12:7-10

> [7] To keep me from becoming conceited because of the surpassingly great revelations, there was given me a thorn in my flesh, a messenger of Satan, to torment me. [8] Three times I pleaded with the Lord to take it away from me. [9] But he said to me, "My grace is sufficient for you, for my power is made perfect in weakness." Therefore I will boast all the more gladly about my weaknesses, so that Christ's power may rest on me. [10] That is why, for Christ's sake, I delight in weaknesses, in insults, in hardships, in persecutions, in difficulties. For when I am weak, then I am strong.

This was a tune that I could not put lyrics to for almost three years. I could only think of the first line. I could not think of the rest of the song. I did know that I wanted to write a love song. The initial thought process came at a soccer game that I was coaching in Cedar Rapids. One of my girls badly sprained her ankle. We did not have a trainer at this game, so I ran out onto the field and carried her off of the field. With tears, she buried her face into my shoulder and tightly wrapped her arms around my neck. At that moment I had the kind of love for all of my players, even my wrestlers, that a father has for his child. I ended up writing this song during my sick leave after my accident. I woke up at 3 a.m. one morning, realizing that I could make this song a love song for *God*. Within two hours after I had made this decision, I had written this and two other songs. The lyrics came naturally and quickly after I had this revelation. Why did I not think of that before? I dunno.

Track 6—Two Are Better Than One

<u>Song of Songs 8:6-7</u>

> [6] Place me like a seal over your heart,
> like a seal on your arm;
> for love is as strong as death,
> its jealousy as unyielding as the grave.
>
> It burns like blazing fire,
> like a mighty flame.
>
> [7] Many waters cannot quench love;
> rivers cannot wash it away
>
> If one were to give
> all the wealth of his house for love,
> it would be utterly scorned.

Ecclesiastes 4:9-12

⁹ Two are better than one,
because they have a good return for their
work:

¹⁰ If one falls down,
his friend can help him up.

But pity the man who falls
and has no one to help him up!

¹¹ Also, if two lie down together, they will
keep warm.

But how can one keep warm alone?

¹² Though one may be overpowered,
two can defend themselves.

A cord of three strands is not quickly broken.

1 Corinthians 13

Karen and I went through a premarital counseling session. We were asked to choose our favorite Bible verses by our counselor. As a wedding present, I decided to write this song for Karen using her favorite verses. (I suppose I am a frugal lover.) This is the song that my friend Keith asked me to play at his wedding. I was honored.

Track 7—Hanging On.

This song really just touches on my frequent lack of willingness to completely trust God, give things completely up to Him, and instead try to do things myself. That has gotten significantly better over the past few years. I did not even intend to put this song on my CD, but my producer convinced me that I should, so I did.

Track 8—Someday

This is a song written for my college roommate and wrestling teammate, "Dieter." Dieter and I had both lived the "women and wine" lifestyle in college. I was certainly not being a strong witness at all. Dieter was a great wrestler and was a very fun kid. Back then I had asked him questions about his beliefs in God. Dieter claimed that he was an atheist. He did not want anything to do with God or any Jesus Christ. He was a year younger than me, so when I got a job teaching in 1994, he still had his senior year to try and win a national title. But that would not come to pass.

Dieter was diagnosed with brain cancer in the fall of 1994 and admitted to a hospital in the town where I lived. That was nice in the sense that I could visit him frequently, which I did. My witnessing efforts became increasingly stronger and more frequent, as Dieter's eternal destination was now the pressing concern – as it should always have been.

On July 4th, 1995, I had plans to get drunk and meet some ladies. I stopped by Dieter's hospital room before I headed off to party. Dieter was dazed and hardly conscious. I sat with him for about twenty minutes before

I patted him on the leg and began to leave. On my way out the door, Dieter murmured, "Goose." He said, "I've been thinking about what you said." I supposed this was a reference to the questions about God. It was a perfect witnessing opportunity. What was my response then? "That's good, Buddy. I'm glad. We'll talk more about it tomorrow." I had drinking to do and women to meet.

The next day I received a phone call. There was no tomorrow. Dieter had passed away during the night. I was beside myself with frustration for putting my pleasure ahead of my friend's eternal salvation.

At his funeral, people got up and spoke about what a party animal he was. I began to think, "Is that the legacy I want to leave?" I spoke about what a legacy was, and what legacy my students wanted to leave behind, and that they should start living as they wanted to be remembered. This fit in nicely when I taught about the legacy of colonialism and FDR's New Deal in various classes. Though my own change in behavior did not really occur until the Promise Keeper's convention in Minneapolis in 1997, this incident reminded me that I needed to change my ways. This song, "Someday," is in memory of "Dieter." It was the first song I ever performed live at church one Sunday, and it received much positive feedback. It is really the song that began the process of creating my first contemporary Christian rock CD.

Track 9—The Trap

John 8:1-11

¹ But Jesus went to the Mount of Olives. ²
At dawn he appeared again in the temple
courts, where all the people gathered around
him, and he sat down to teach them. ³The
teachers of the law and the Pharisees brought
in a woman caught in adultery. They made her
stand before the group ⁴ and said to Jesus,
"Teacher, this woman was caught in the act
of adultery. ⁵ In the Law Moses commanded
us to stone such women. Now what do you
say?" ⁶ They were using this question as a
trap, in order to have a basis for accusing him.

But Jesus bent down and started to write on
the ground with his finger. ⁷ When they kept
on questioning him, he straightened up and
said to them, "If any of you is without sin,
let him be the first to throw a stone at her."
⁸ Again he stooped down and wrote on the
ground.

⁹ At this, those who heard began to go away
one at a time, the older ones first, until only
Jesus was left, with the woman still standing
there. ¹⁰ Jesus straightened up and asked
her, "Woman, where are they? Has no one
condemned you?"

¹¹ "No one, sir," she said.

"Then neither do I condemn you," Jesus
declared. "Go now and leave your life of sin."

This and the Prodigal Son (Luke 15:11-32) are my two favorite Bible stories, because I feel like they are both speaking directly to me. It seems as though I am the Prodigal Son *and* I am the woman in John 8:1-11. I must continually recall that Jesus' blood has forgiven my sin, just as the woman and the Prodigal Son were forgiven.

Track 10—Coming of Age

<u>John 8:31-32</u>

> [31] To the Jews who had believed him, Jesus said, "If you hold to my teaching, you are really my disciples. [32] Then you will know the truth, and the truth will set you free."

The lyrics of this song and John 8:31-32 are fairly self-explanatory. I suppose this song could be an anthem for this book.

Track 11—Praying For Keeps

This song is not inspired by any particular scriptures. This was the very first Christian song that I ever wrote. I conceived of this as a prayer to God.

Track 12—Those Like You

<u>Galatians 2:15-21</u>

> [15] "We who are Jews by birth and not 'Gentile sinners' [16] know that a man is not justified by

observing the law, but by faith in Jesus Christ. So we, too, have put our faith in Christ Jesus that we may be justified by faith in Christ and not by observing the law, because by observing the law no one will be justified.

[17] "If, while we seek to be justified in Christ, it becomes evident that we ourselves are sinners, does that mean that Christ promotes sin? Absolutely not! [18] If I rebuild what I destroyed, I prove that I am a lawbreaker. [19] For through the law I died to the law so that I might live for God. [20] I have been crucified with Christ and I no longer live, but Christ lives in me. The life I live in the body, I live by faith in the Son of God, who loved me and gave himself for me. [21] I do not set aside the grace of God, for if righteousness could be gained through the law, Christ died for nothing!"

"Those Like You" was written shortly after the former pastor from my previous church spoke in my class in 1997. It is really about the dueling personalities within myself; the "professor man" who thinks he has all of the answers versus the humble Christian. It seemed that Galatians 2:16-21 touched a bit on the message that I was trying to portray in this song: we are not redeemed through our works, but rather the blood of Jesus alone. This was another one of the first songs I performed live and people seemed to like it. As a huge fan of wrestling, I was very pleased when Tom Brands, the head coach of the Iowa Hawkeyes, was visiting our church the day I performed this song after he had won a gold medal in the 1996 Olympics. He came up to me and said, "I thoroughly enjoyed that song." Iowa wrestling seems to be back to its winning ways and it is nice to see a strong Christian at the helms. The results are living proof.

If you are interested in MP3s of my songs, they are available online at http://cdbaby.com/cd/troylangos.

My CD cover.
Symbolic of new life.

I eventually gave the last of my CDs to my natural chiropractor and his staff. He plays guitar, himself, and I think he may also have been in a band in his younger days. After listening to my CD, he suggested that I start a non-profit organization in which I could play my music and tell my story. He believed that this would speak to many people. I thought that this sounded interesting, but the fact that I could no longer play my guitar would make it hard to do. (I will touch on later in this book.) If I could find some people to be my background band, that might work, but most people have full-time jobs and families. Unless I knew that this would become a full-time job, I was not willing to take that risk, as I have a family of my own to think about. In my early twenties, touring for Christ would have seemed like an exciting endeavor, but now I did not think this was the time to gamble with my family's well-being.

Chapter 7

For Better <u>and</u> For Worse

Due to the injuries from my accident in 2001, I had been unable to lift weights at all for about a year. After being diagnosed with Multiple Sclerosis, my initial vision and fatigue problems subsided after a couple of months. Through physical therapy I began to improve my strength. My therapist worked for a professional hockey team. He was harsh and aggressive and I loved it! He knew how to get an athlete back into competing form, and that is more or less what I wanted from him. He was great! I began stretching and lifting soup cans as weights – for which the gym rats at the club poked a whole lot of fun at me, as you can imagine. Through the course of therapy from October 2001 to December 2002, I got back to where I could bench press 295 pounds and felt pretty good. But life would again take another abrupt U-turn. Some of the change was wonderful, some was horrible.

Karen and I had decided in the spring of 2002 that we thought we were ready for a child. Not much later she got pregnant. On December 6, 2002, our daughter was born. I was hesitant to watch the delivery, but when that beautiful little head popped out, it was the coolest thing I have ever witnessed in my entire life. I would recommend watching the delivery for all daddies, even if they believe they are too weak to stomach it. It was very cool! When my daughter came out of the womb she had her umbilical cord wrapped around her neck, so doctors swiftly placed her on a table to take care of her. She was crying boisterously. The doctor let me stand at the head of the table at which they were working while Karen recouped. With a bit of worry I softly spoke to the new baby. "It'll be alright, Honey. It'll be alright." I had sung to, spoken to, and read to my daughter while she was still in the womb. That must have served its purpose, because just as I uttered those soft words, she stopped crying and looked back up over her shoulder to see where the voice was coming from. She must have recognized my voice. She had my lifelong commitment from that moment. It was the sweetest thing in the world and words cannot do it justice. It melted my heart. She would be okay and grow up to be a beautiful, wonderful child. Karen and I were truly blessed and we thank God for her every single day of our lives. That was the great news.

Daughter and Dad in her very early years

But I was soon to receive news that was not so great. While working out at the health club over Christmas break only a couple of weeks later, I stepped off of the elliptical machine to head for the showers. My legs suddenly felt heavy and lethargic. I am not talking about the fatigue I was feeling from a 20-minute session on the elliptical machine, I am talking about a heaviness that I had never experienced in my lifetime. I could hardly lift my legs to walk and had to use the wall to assist myself to the bench in the locker room, where I rested and considered what to do next.

This continued for the next six months with some good days and some bad days. I continued to pray for wisdom and discretion for my health situation. But with tear-stained eyes, I sat down with Karen one afternoon to discuss the possibility of me spending the rest of my life in a wheelchair. We decided that we would sell our split-foyer home and move to a ranch house that would not require me to negotiate stairs.

In June, my wife unintentionally happened upon a website from a naturalist. He claimed that I would see some improvement within 90 days if I was committed to the homeostasis protocol that he outlined. He was careful not to guarantee healing within 90 days, but he promised that improvements would occur.

I called him, and the first thing I asked about was his faith. I was impressed and pleased to hear, not that he was a Christian – as that can mean so many different things to different people – but that he had a close and personal relationship with Jesus Christ. He, himself, had cancer and was given months to live over 25 years ago. He told me what I could likely expect physically and, regardless of my illness, that I needed to get my body into an alkaline state in which no disease could survive. I likely had had this disease for years. The symptoms were probably triggered by the head trauma from my car accident in 2001. Thus, I needed to be patient, as it would likely take years of commitment to this homeostasis protocol to feel "healed." For the next year I progressed just as the naturalist said that I would if were faithful. I was faithful and I did progress nicely.

I started to feel fairly normal. I mean, I was not going

to run a marathon or anything, but walks with my family and day-to-day activities were no problem. I do not know why, but I started to "play God" and "cheat" at times. The humidity of an Iowa summer zapped me now and then, and so I used this as justification for my next foolish decision.

I had stumbled across information through readings and testimonies about Lyme disease. It appeared that every single one of my symptoms matched up. Lyme disease is known as the "great imitator" because it manifests itself as symptoms from other chronic illnesses. The top three most commonly misdiagnosed diseases that are actually Lyme disease are Fibromyalgia, Chronic Fatigue, and Multiple Sclerosis. One of the top five Lyme disease specialists in the entire United States, and the closest of the top specialists to me, carried on his practice in Springfield, Missouri. He claimed that most hospitals make mistakes with the blood test for Lyme disease because they do not follow proper methods for blood testing for that disease. Well, I did not want to get my hopes up too much, but I made the eight-hour drive to Springfield to at least exhaust the possibility. After weeks of anticipation the results came back. Sure enough, I had Lyme disease.

If a "bull's eye" rash from a tick bite is noticed right away, antibiotics can quickly heal this disease. But this could have been in my bloodstream for 30 years, and antibiotics don't work so well for chronic Lyme disease. I found this out the hard way and started oral antibiotics. The doctor claimed that after significant and continual improvement I would be healed within 9-12 months on an antibiotic regimen. The first thing I had to do was pray about this, as antibiotics completely contradicted the natural protocol I was already on. I prayed for about three weeks and continued to feel a conviction to forget about the antibiotics and stay on the natural protocol. I became convicted at church one Sunday morning that I would never put an antibiotic into my body. But the certainty from that conviction somehow was overturned within two hours. I somehow decided that people in my life, my doctor, and pretty much everyone in the world knew more about my health situation than the Creator of the universe. Going against that continual conviction that I should stick with the natural protocol, I began the antibiotic regimen. I took antibiotics and hormone treatments to maximize the antibiotics for four and a half months. I did not improve significantly. In fact, for some reason I was lucky to get two to four hours of sleep each night, which was an unanticipated and unwelcome side-effect to say the least. Sleeplessness had not been a problem since I started the homeostasis protocol over a year earlier. I decided that I would rather be in a wheelchair than not sleep. The sleeplessness was horrible and made me completely non-functional – not to mention making me very difficult for my wife to live with, I am certain. But she is so sweet that she would probably never mention that to anyone even if you asked her.

The entire time I was taking antibiotics and hormone medication, I still felt that conviction to stay natural, but I continued to give the antibiotics "the old college try" in hope of a quick recovery. After four and a half months the sleeplessness was too much to handle, and I felt as if God was literally smacking me upside of my thick skull. It was as if He was saying, *"You asked for guidance and wisdom. I have been giving it to you for months and you are still trying to do things your way. Wake up, Troy!"* Ironically, I *couldn't* sleep, and yet it seemed like God was telling me to *"wake up."* Was that a sign? I do not have any idea, but after deciding to halt my antibiotic regiment and go back on the homeostasis protocol, I asked my Heavenly Father for forgiveness and for wisdom about how to correct my wrongs.

On a side note, it would be another three years before I realized one big mistake I had been making, probably THE major mistake. With the help of my wonderful wife, I later realized that God gave us medicine. Proverbs 17:22 says *"A cheerful heart is good medicine."* So be happy. That is very important. Yes, God also gave us doctors: Luke was a physician. The mistake I had been making was putting my hope for complete healing in those doctors and remedies and not putting my trust in God.

Rather than obeying God and His original prompting for me to go the natural route, I had been taken in by the promise of a quick fix, and I knew that through the blood of Christ I had already been forgiven for that. But I also knew that did *not* mean that there would be no consequences for my disobedience. I called to confess to my naturalist and to figure out what I could do to detoxify and restart my healing process all over again. It was reassuring that he did not verbally beat me up about my decision with a chorus of "I told you so, I told you so, I told you so." It was also reassuring when he reminded me that this disease could have been in my bloodstream for years and that there would be nothing like a quick fix to recover from it. It may take years of dedication to recover. So I started the homeostasis protocol once again.

Since I made that decision I *have* struggled physically, but actually I have been spiritually and emotionally strong. Like my Dad had said when I was first diagnosed with MS, my friends and family continued to ask me how I can stay upbeat and trust and praise God through all of this. My response has always been the same: Sometimes I feel like God is the ONLY one I can trust, and that He is the ONLY one worthy of my praise.

I had always been a little bit confused about which disease I actually had. Both my Lyme disease doctor and my MS doctors are convinced that I had one disease and not the other. My MS doctor even did a blood test for Lyme disease on me. I tested positive for one band of Lyme disease, but one needs to test positive for two bands of Lyme disease for a positive diagnosis. Thus, my MS doctor said that I was negative for Lyme. So I still see my MS neurologist every three months to chart my status and take a medicine that does not heal, but which slows the progression of the disease. I see that medicine as a good thing regardless of which disease I have.

However, I did not want to ignore the fact that a reputable doctor diagnosed me with Lyme disease. I searched for ways to naturally treat the disease. I stumbled across a treatment by something called a Rife machine. The Rife machine was developed in the 1930's by Raymond Rife and is primarily used by Lyme disease victims. It restructures the cells in your body by sending out electronic waves. It really helps some people. It really did *not* help me. I took my Rife machine into a chiropractor for some tests. The chiropractor did some muscle reflex tests on me using certain frequencies. I tested positive for twelve Lyme disease frequencies and zero MS frequencies. As I mentioned before, Lyme disease is known as the "great imitator," even down to the plaques on your brain from an MRI. So these things make me lean toward thinking that I have Lyme disease – or I wonder if it is possible that I have *both* diseases. Health insurance will not cover much for Lyme disease, and most people do not understand how serious it can be or even what it is. So, I generally tell people that I have MS, and then no questions or doubts arise.

I do have one interesting and frustrating health insurance story. I have a friend down the street who had been diagnosed with Fibromyalgia and was having a very difficult time with it. She also got tested for Lyme disease and tested positive. She began taking IV antibiotics and the results were like night and day. She is doing great. IV antibiotics cost about $9,000 per month. So I called my health insurance company to see if this would be covered. They said that they would cover 90% and that I would be responsible for the rest. That is still expensive, but if I had the same results as my friend, it would be well worth it. Three weeks into my IV treatment, I received a letter from my insurance company telling me that they would *not* cover *any* of the IV antibiotics. At this point, if that is the case, then I am in deep – more than $6,000 deep. I also have another friend who is an attorney, so I called her and told her my story and asked if she could write the insurance company a letter. She agreed that she would. The insurance company must have gotten scared, because they did not charge me one penny. I was willing to pay the 10% they said I would be responsible for, but 0% was sure nice. From that incident I learned to *always get things in writing*, and I was reminded again how great our God is. Unfortunately, my Lyme disease doctor (who was a wonderful Christian man) had to call me during this experience to tell me that he could no longer see me and that I should find a local doctor. My insurance company had been calling him and, in his own words, "harassing" him, and he did not want to put up with that anymore.

Valley Church

All that business about diagnoses and treatments and health insurance was only one part of what went on those years. During all of that, at the church that I had attended for almost nine years, one of the pastors was asked to step down because, as some members of the congregation were told, he gave "unbiblical counsel" to one member of the congregation. In actuality, there had been some difference of opinion between elders, some of the other pastors, and this particular pastor about how one would define "Biblical counsel." Essentially, this was little more than a rumor spread within the congregation. This other pastor was not necessarily asked to leave and, with shrugged shoulders, the church board was left questioning what they should now do. I do not know all of what happened, so perhaps I am the one spreading rumors now. That is not my intention, and I love and am good friends with all of the pastors at that church. There are some wonderful things said from the pulpit there. But I also loved this Godly pastor and friend who, as much of the congregation at that church thought, was asked to step down. My wife Karen worked as a bookkeeper and secretary at that church, and she considered that pastor's wife one of her best friends. So when that pastor left our old church to plant a new church, I was between a rock and a hard place about what to do. My wife wanted to follow her friend and her pastor husband, and so we did. They ended up finding an old restaurant that had closed down – a place that I had heard was once a speakeasy. The intriguing thing to me was that this old restaurant and bar was now a church.

The summer of 2005 would bring me even more heartache. That summer was very hot and dry, and my illness took a drastic turn for the worse at the end of June. I was out watering the flowers and shrubs in my yard that day, when suddenly I just dropped to my knees. I literally could not hold myself up. I had to crawl over to turn off the faucet, and then crawled into the house. Heat had never bothered me before. Lying on the couch in the air conditioning was about all that I could do the rest of that summer – and every summer since.

This happened on a Tuesday, and I was supposed to sing and play guitar at two of my former students' wedding that Saturday. Unfortunately, this was also the end of my guitar playing, because for some reason my fingers could not grip the chords on my guitar. I have not been able to play my guitar since. (For that same reason, I have to "hunt and peck" while I am typing this book.) I don't know how to explain the problem. My chiropractor gave me a grip test, and my grip was apparently stronger than many of his patients. I just know that I cannot type or play my guitar, and my grip and fingers feel weak. "Significantly decreased dexterity" would probably be a better description of the problem. Whatever you call it, that week I had to call my former students and tell them about my predicament, and that I could not play "Love Song for A Savior" by Jars of Clay at their wedding that weekend. I had just played that song at church the past weekend, so I knew it well, but my fingers would not cooperate. My former students were so kind and gracious to me, saying that my health was more important and that they understood. Many people would probably not have been so nice about it. The programs had already been printed up, and there was my name and the title of the song I would be playing. As you can imagine, some folks asked why Mr. Langos was not playing like the program said.

A month after that, I was also supposed to stand up for a very good friend at a courtyard wedding in Los Angeles. This was a man that I wrestled with in high school, and I was looking forward to being there for him.

Besides, Karen and I were looking forward to a bit of romance for ourselves, without our daughter along. Well, we couldn't go. From what I heard, the brother of the groom said some very touching things about the fact that I, and more importantly, his Dad who had just recently passed away, could not be at the wedding. During the ceremony, My friend left an empty space where I was to stand. I was very touched by that gesture.

The final thing Karen and I missed was a trip to Houston to see her aunt and uncle, who are both wonderful folks. I was looking forward to seeing them. So why did we miss all of these fun experiences? My neurologist said that there is no way that I should be in Los Angeles or Texas in August given my recent condition. Of course I cannot wait for anything, so days after I found out about my friend Brian's wedding back in December, Karen and I also decided to go to see her Aunt and Uncle, and I had purchased $2000 worth of airline tickets. Thanks to 9/11, airline tickets could no longer be transferred to someone else, not even with a doctor's excuse.

I have never really recovered from that summer's physical setbacks. I do continue to work out as much as I can, but the days of intense workouts are over. I now work out with 15 and 20 pound dumbbells, do sit-ups and push-ups, stretch, and do physical therapy exercises for leg strength. I do these three times a week, which is about all that I can muster. As my illness progresses, this gets increasingly difficult, but even if this is all that I can do, I need to stay as active as I can.

The thing that brought me down the most that summer was watching through the window as my wife Karen mowed the lawn and played with our daughter outside. I thought, "That should be what the man of the house does, not my beautiful and delicate wife." The next summer I set my penny-pinching mindset aside and agreed to hire a lawn service to mow the grass. One day that summer, while I was lying in the air conditioning and looking out, I saw tiny little lip and finger prints on the glass on the door to the outside. I lost it and began sobbing. I believe I was thinking about life for Karen and my daughter without a Daddy or a husband.

Dad and daughter at a Sesame Street Live production

Chapter 8

A Bittersweet Surrender

My daughter is a constant source of laughter and joy in our family. Sometimes, a stretch of time will go by when she is the only thing I have to laugh about. Ever since she started speaking, I have written down memorable and funny things she has said. Most of them I was in tears laughing when she said them, a few were not so much funny, just unbelievable that she said them. For example, when she was three, I drew her attention to the sky, where the sun was beautiful like I had rarely seen. What was my daughter's reaction? "That's amazing!" I had never taught her that word, but it was so cute in that context. What follows here are a few of my young daughter's hilarious quotes. Like the goofy things my friends and I said or did, you may not find them as funny as I do.

At a restaurant, my wife needed to excuse herself. While she was gone, her dessert came. My daughter asked

Daddy getting an "I love you" from daughter

if she could have a bite and I told her that I did not think that Mom would mind, so she took a bite. I asked, "How was it?"

My daughter responded, "That was *ferocious!*"

To my knowledge, I had never used that word around her, so I asked, "What do you mean?"

"It was good, it was tasty."

"That's what I thought you meant," I chuckled.

That word worked so well in that moment that I asked my daughter if I could use it like that. She said that I had her permission to use that word in that context. I knew that she would.

On another occasion, my wife and I were driving through downtown just as University classes were starting around Labor Day weekend. My daughter was sitting in the back seat while two boys were walking by without shirts on. My wife said, "That's not very modest is it, Honey?"

Daddy and daughter at the park

My daughter responded, "Maybe they're having a no-shirt fiesta." She must have learned the word "fiesta" from

Dora the Explorer or something, but not from us. We all laughed.

Once, Karen must have said something to our daughter about the dangers of taking a small toy to bed with her, and she put it on the dresser out of my daughter's reach. First thing the next morning, my little girl points at the toy and says, "Can I have that choking hazard?"

My daughter had three bookmarks and wanted to know which one to use for a book that she had. Karen told her to just do eenie-meenie-mynie-moe to choose one. After a few seconds, my daughter held up a bookmark and asked "What do I do with this one?" Karen responded that she should just use that one for a bookmark in another book. My daughter said, "But it was not '*it*.'"

Just recently we were on a trip to North Carolina, and my daughter was very excited about her first trip on an airplane. Upon taking off, we got just above the clouds and she said to my wife "Look! We're above the clouds!" My wife mentioned to my daughter "Ya know, when Jesus returns, He's going to ride on a cloud?" My daughter exclaims in response "He TOTALLY ROCKS!"

My daughter was enthusiastic at take-off, but upon landing a few hours later and feeling a bit nauseous, she said "Mom? I am the type of person who likes to stay on the ground."

And finally, seeing the trouble the lawn mowing

service was having mowing around my trees, I made a comment to my daughter that I needed to trim the branches on those trees. She said that she could do it if I told her how. I told her that I would have to point out which branches to trim, and then she would have to trim those branches with the clippers and then put those branches in a bag for disposal. Her response was, "I can do that. That's hysterically easy!"

As you can see, our daughter is a constant source of wonder and humor for both me and Karen. We are truly blessed.

Around October of 2006, my friend Chad called me to ask if I would be offended if he had a fundraiser for me to help pay for all of the medical bills that I had been accruing. I told him I did not know why he thought that I would ever be offended by such a kind and thoughtful gesture, so he did have a fundraiser for me at his house. I am so proud of Chad. He has literally worked himself into a top home builder in Des Moines. Many of his well-to-do business clients and contacts came to the fundraiser – probably out of courtesy to him and not out of any interest in me. I did not know many of the people at this fundraiser, but I was thrilled to see some old friends that I had not seen since high school. Chad had wonderful food and live music. It was not only nice of him, but very exquisite and a lot of fun.

The morning before the fundraiser, my family and some friends, including Chad and Jeff, watched some football and talked. I was using a cane at that time and Jeff decided I needed a nickname for my cane. He dubbed my cane with the name "Chewy," which my daughter got a kick out of, even though she had never seen *Star Wars*.

Karen and I had decided we would tithe ten percent of whatever was raised, even though I am not sure whether one is supposed to tithe gifts. It just seemed like the right thing to do. I had been learning more and more about tithing. Karen and I had always given ten percent since we got married, but in that ten percent we included whatever we gave to charities, Christian radio stations or the like. We later came to realize that ten percent should go to the local church, the "storehouse," and that everything else should be considered offerings above the tithe.

Malachi 3:9-12 says:

> [9] "You are under a curse – the whole nation of you – because you are robbing me. [10] Bring the whole tithe into the storehouse, that there may be food in my house. Test me in this," says the Lord Almighty, "and see if I will not throw open the floodgates of heaven and pour out so much blessing that you will not have room enough for it. [11] I will prevent pests from devouring your crops, and the vines of your fields will not cast their fruit," says the Lord Almighty, [12] "Then all the

nations will call you blessed, for yours will be
a delightful land," says the Lord Almighty.

Since Karen and I started tithing as we are supposed
to, we have seen God throw open the floodgates of heaven
upon us. I would recommend that everyone test God in
this as He says in Malachi. I am not saying that if you
tithe you will become a millionaire, but you will lack little
and you will be blessed. And who knows, maybe you *will*
become a millionaire. But do not tithe with the wrong
attitude. Chad's fundraiser raised enough to completely
pay off my medical bills, tithe ten percent to the local
church, *and* have $20 left over for a good start on a date
with Karen.

As I mentioned, Karen and I always gave ten percent
to God in various ways, just not necessarily to our local
church. We gave to Campus Crusade for Christ, Christian
Children's fund, the local Christian school, and the local
Christian radio station, as well as to the local church. Now
that we know more about what tithing should be, we still
give to these other things listed above, but we consider
these offerings above and beyond the tithe – and God is
still blessing us by keeping away any financial worries.

Earlier in August of 2006, I had sung the Casting
Crowns song "Praise You in This Storm" at church. In light
of the physical ailments that I had been going through,

that song had become my anthem. I love it. I cried the first two times I heard it on the car stereo, and I still get a bit choked up from time to time when I hear it. Our pastor at our new church asked me to sing that song at least once a month. By November, I believed that the congregation and I needed a break. Pastor Paul had his own physical problems. He had diabetes, could not see well at all (and could not drive as a result), and he had kidney problems. But he was one of the more Godly and inspirational men that I knew, and I could not believe that he had been asked to leave our old church. I told Paul I wanted to take a break from singing that song in November. Paul ended up having a stroke and dying late that November. I guess I could have sung the song one more time.

I had a friend at work named Jim, who was an avid bicycler and one of our tech specialists at the school. Being the computer moron that I had become, I would have been lost without him. Jim came up to me one day during my open hour. I was sitting in my wheelchair, and he asked me how I could remain so "upbeat" given my circumstances. He mentioned how active I used to be, and now I was in a wheelchair with a smile on my face. Jim said that he needed knee surgery and was not sure if he would be able to bicycle anymore, and that he was pretty downhearted because of this. He just wanted to know what gave *me* joy. My response came without hesitation:

"Jesus." I took a minute to briefly tell him about what Jesus had done in my life.

In situations like this, I cannot help but remember 2 Corinthians 1:3-5, which reads:

> 3 **"Praise be to the God and Father of our Lord Jesus Christ, the Father of compassion and the God of all comfort, 4 who comforts us in all our troubles, so that we can comfort those in any trouble with the comfort we ourselves have received from God. 5 For just as the sufferings of Christ flow over into our lives, so also through Christ our comfort overflows."**

Those verses make me realize that God can find a purpose in all things and can use any situation for good. Perhaps my words were a comfort to my friend.

The next day, Jim was admitted to the hospital with a kidney infection. Having seen what had happened with Pastor Paul's kidney problems, I knew how serious that could have been. This gentleman spent a week in the hospital. When he returned, I paid him a visit and asked him, "Did your frightening experience change your views about things?" Jim said that he had decided to start eating right. "No, no," I said, "Did your views change about God?" He said that it really had not changed his views about God. I would say that my odds are probably about one in ten or more in favor of leading people to Christ when I witness to them, but that still means there are a few more people who know Christ who did not know Him before. So I don't let those odds discourage me from trying to witness whenever I can. Do not ever let improbable odds keep you from witnessing.

After Pastor Paul went home to the Lord in November 2006, the search for a new pastor at Valley Church began. In the meantime, several men from the congregation were asked to rotate preaching each Sunday until a new pastor was hired. I was one of the men asked to preach and I did preach three times, which I thoroughly enjoyed. I even sang "Praise You in This Storm" in one of my sermons – dedicating it to Paul, of course. The first sermon that I had planned I ended up changing a few days before that Sunday, because I found out that my parents were coming up to see Karen, their granddaughter, and me *and* that they were planning on going to church with us.

Dad was coming back to the Lord and that excited me. About six months earlier he had sent me a card. As he was a man of few words, all that the card said was this: "As your father, your illness is killing me. But you have been an inspiration through your attitude in all that you are going through. If anyone has brought me close to God again, it's you."

Praise God! That was one of the nicest, most encouraging things anybody could have written to me.

And the whole "back to God again" comment made me think that perhaps he was just backslidden for most of my life. The only unforgivable sin is to deny God. And that is only unforgivable if it is a continual pattern, not an infrequent happening. Even Peter denied Jesus three times and was later known as the cornerstone of the Christian church and was called "The Rock." So I am sure Dad has been forgiven for his backsliding, just as I have been.

Dad has started going to church again and has even become the finance director at his church. He is doing Bible studies, reading the Bible, and praying again. I am thrilled that he is making God a part of his life again.

But Dad still needs to work on his relationship with his other son, my brother Shane. When I found out Mom and Dad were visiting my family and planning on coming to our church, I changed my sermon to speak directly to him. My new sermon would deal with 1 John 4:7-21, which begins with:

> [7] Dear friends, let us love one another, for love comes from God. Everyone who loves has been born of God and knows God.

And that section ends with:

> [19] We love because he first loved us. [20] If anyone says, "I love God," yet hates his brother, he is a liar. For anyone who does not love his brother, whom he has seen, cannot

love God, whom he has not seen. ²¹ And he
has given us this command: Whoever loves
God must also love his brother.

My hope was that this message would sink into Dad's stubborn mindset and that, no matter who might be wrong in their relationship, he would initiate a peace gesture to my brother and the rest of the family, reconciling these relationships. It would be so wonderful to have just *one* Christmas, *one* Thanksgiving, *one* Easter, and *one* birthday party for my daughter again, instead of one with Mom and Dad and another with the rest of the family.

When I asked Dad what he thought of the service, his response was that there were a few good songs. I asked, "What did you think of my sermon, Dad?" He responded that he wasn't really listening to that. Was he kidding? Did he really not listen to his son's first sermon? Or was he just hiding behind some sort of guilt and did not want to admit it? I am really not sure.

We finally hired a new pastor, who started preaching at Valley church in June of 2007. Ajai and his wife, Maureena, are both from India. They had met Pastor Paul while Ajai was at seminary out East, and they also had family connections in our area. I did not know if I would ever know a man with greater faith than Paul had, but Ajai is right up there.

Pastor Ajai came from the Kshatriya (warrior) caste, but despite the Hindu caste and even though his grandparents were indeed Hindu, he was fortunate to come from one of the few families in India that are Christian. At the age of 14 months, Ajai miraculously survived a life-threatening medical condition, and his parents then dedicated him to a life of service to God. Ajai and Maureena ended up living in the Middle East for several years and then moved to Boston, where Ajai went to seminary. The night of November 29, 2006, Ajai could not sleep. God had told him he was to shepherd Valley Church in Iowa. Ajai did not know why and he certainly was not terribly excited about moving to Iowa, but he would listen to God's calling. Paul passed away the next day, and now Ajai understood the events of the previous evening. After the interview process at Valley Church and upon finishing seminary in May, he was hired and started as the new pastor in June of 2007. Pastor Ajai would not and did not even accept a salary until the church could get out of debt. This went on for several months, but the church trustees – one of whom is my beautiful wife – ended up insisting that he get paid something, so he eventually began to receive a very minimal salary.

Maureena looked for a job as a nurse and ended up getting a better job than she thought she might as the director of nursing at Lantern Park Nursing Center. She is the one who convinced me to write this autobiography and to have my CD readily available upon request. I did not know what was so special about my life, but it sounded like a good idea. Eventually you will see why I have had extra time to write this book.

Karen and I happily serve at Valley Church today. Karen still serves on the trustee board and does all of the church bookwork. I serve on the advisory board and am on the church praise team. In regards to my being on the praise team, I was recently told an encouraging story about a church member who had to have hip surgery and had to walk with crutches. When this gentleman was asked if he hated being on crutches, he responded (in reference to me) that he could not complain because he could still walk. He continued, "Troy always has to use a walker or a wheelchair, and yet every week that he can, he hobbles onto stage with a smile." That was refreshing to hear and makes me realize how important a positive attitude can be.

On another side note, I have been attending a Bible study at Pastor Ajai's home every other Friday night for awhile. Sometimes I looked for excuses not to go, but I always ended up being glad that I did go. The study is about spiritual warfare. One night, Leviticus 19:28 came up in our reading. It says: *"Do not cut your bodies for the dead or put tattoo marks on yourselves. I am the Lord."* I was interested in Leviticus 19:28 because I had two tattoos. One is on my right thigh so it could be seen when I wore my wrestling singlet and I have one on my right upper arm of my college rock band's "mascot." I had gotten them both because I thought they would make me look cool, but I wish I had never gotten either one of them. I had the tattoos done in my younger, wilder days, and Pastor Ajai assured me that since I got these before I made Christ my Lord, God loved me nonetheless and forgave me for them. I do not think, however, that does not mean that there will be no consequences for something God commanded us to not do. I am not sure what those consequences may be.

Working

In April of 2006, I was visited by my principal to discuss some comments that had been made by some students and/or parents about my classes. I had been having some mental clarity issues – things like concentration, focus, and even communication becoming quite a struggle at times. Unable to walk more than a few feet (even with a walker), I had been forced to teach in a wheelchair. I could still teach effectively in a wheelchair. Many teachers do. Being in a wheelchair was not ideal, but it did not bother me as I thought it might. But I did have to admit to the principal that I was having mental clarity issues, and I further pointed out that for some reason those issues did not become a problem until after noon. The principal thus agreed that I would go on half-time disability for the rest of the year, which was about 60 days.

The next year I seemed to be doing much better, so I started to work full-time again. I received the most treasured email from a student that February, 2007. She was a senior in my World Religions class. In that class, in such a liberal school and community (for Iowa, of course), I mostly enjoyed teaching about Christianity. When the students asked questions about Christianity, I answered with Bible scriptures just as Jesus did to Satan when tempted by him in the wilderness (Matthew 4:1-11, Luke 4:1-13), and I also asked students to please not take the Lord's name in vain whenever they did ask about Him. I explained that it would be as offensive to someone as calling a black person the "N" word. But I never preached to my students. So apart from asking students not to take the Lord's name in vain or being a living witness (which I was not as much as I should have been), I do not know what prompted one comment in this girl's email. Nonetheless, I still have her note and I always will. That email and Dad's card are the most inspiring things that I have ever received. The email said:

Mr. Langos-

Ashley __ here! I just wanted to thank you for this trimester. Truthfully, this has been my favorite class I've ever taken. You truly are a wonderful teacher and I'm so thankful for having been in your class. Through your class I've gained insight in which I've never had and now I feel like a more worldly person. I'm kind of embarrassed to say this, but before your class I used to say and do things that the Lord does not approve of and now I have found that I don't do those things anymore. And I have come to respect and have a deeper understanding of other people's perspectives and beliefs. So thanks again and keep up the great work.

Sincerely, Ashley __

I have received other nice cards, letters, and comments from students in the past. I have two binders full of them. I have some wonderful gifts and CD compilations of students' favorite songs from Japan, China, India, Southeast Asia, and all around the world. All of them are nice, but this email from Ashley really pulled on my heart strings. It is the kind of thing that teachers really enjoy about their job.

The next October, 2007, I had a girl come in to drop my class and uttered some fairly unkind and disrespectful words, but that is also part of the job. Many kids today do not have proper upbringing or father-figures in their lives, and I understand that and deal with it as best I can. Teachers are *"in loco parentis"* and must be at times. The thing that confused me is what happened next.

Less than one week later, the principal came into my room to talk to me during my open hour. Right off the bat he asked me if I read the Bible in class. I told him that I never read it to students, but if they were working in the computer lab or independently working in class, and if nobody had any questions about what they had been assigned, I told him that I occasionally did read the Bible in class. He reminded me that during times like those, I was to work on lesson plans, not to engage in any personal things. He was pretty nice about it, and he was right and I did know better. He then started talking about what a disengaged teacher I had become.

I intend no disrespect by writing the things that will follow, but this is where my perspective comes in. I do not know the specifics about the bad comments he received about me, no more than he knew about the *good* comments I had received from students and parents in conferences or via comments, letters, cards, or emails. I understand that. It just seemed interesting that this conversation took place less than a week after this student dropped my class. Did a parent call and ream him out and say that I was not a very good teacher? I suspect that is what happened. I looked back through the lesson plans for all five of my classes and they were very good. There was, however, a six-day period between units when I was handing out a lot of in-class work and was not being very actively engaged. That was the class that this girl was in, and the end of that six-day period is when she dropped my class. I could see her point. So I ended up getting twelve new lessons from the library, online, and from co-workers that were pretty solid. I usually did this for one or two lessons for each class each trimester. I turned in the lessons to the principal and his response after weeks was simply, "Thanks." There was no comment on the lessons looking good or anything, but I know that he is a very busy man and probably had better things to do than address my new lessons in detail.

In January of 2008, I had my Career Teacher Assessment meeting. I got the highest marks that I could on everything except being an "engaged teacher," where I got poor marks. I did find this interesting in light of concluding comments he made on my past three classroom observations, the last being about a week or two before the incident when the student dropped my class. I only have my last three evaluations, but I do recall that in fifteen years of teaching they had all being quite favorable. The principal's concluding comments on my in-class evaluations follow:

October 18, 2004

Classroom Management:

The teacher projects a professional and organized image. He has good relationships with students and use of time in class was used in a purposeful fashion. We also talked about the process of getting kids into groups in an expeditious manner. The observer recognized the teacher uses a variety of approaches in having such a learning activity processed. The teacher indicated through his professional growth he has modified some of his presentation of content to students moving more to a collaborative approach as compared to a lecture format.

December 13, 2004

Classroom Management:

The class was conducted in an orderly fashion with all students actively and positively engaged in the lesson.

October 22, 2007

Classroom Management:

All students were actively engaged throughout the lesson. The teacher's enthusiasm and verbal engagement of students through a variety of questions also helped support a successful lesson.

I also give end-of-course evaluations to students for my own personal development. I tell students not to put their names on the surveys because I want their sincere comments about what they did or did not like and to let me know if I am an engaged teacher. All but one student out of more than 250 students for the year 2007-2008 said that I was an engaged teacher and that they learned something new in my class. Between student survey feedback, positive student and parental feedback, and my administrative evaluations, how could I think anything but that my teaching was still engaged and useful?

In the year 2008-2009, I was not able to teach my favorite class, World Religions, which I had taught for 12 years and which had developed quite nicely. It was instead given to a 22-year-old who was fresh out of college. She was a good teacher, but why did the administration give this class to her and not me? When my wife asked the administration about this, she was told that it was because of reorganizing class offerings. Why was I not told this, and why did I not have some seniority after 15 years? That year I also had to turn in lesson plans for *all* of my classes for the week, which was unexpected but did not really violate my contract. In fact, most teachers in the state of Iowa have to do that, but no other teachers in my building had to. I also started having "drop-in" visits by administrators a couple of times per week. Again, none of this violated the contract, but my drop-ins were much more frequent than any other teacher in the building, and nobody else seemed to be going through this level of scrutiny in my building. It did not seem fair and it was stressing me out, which was not at all good for my health.

I finally asked three teachers from my department if they would come and observe me during their open hours, to see if the scrutiny and criticism was valid, or if, as I thought, I was just being unfairly set up for failure. They all agreed.

I am good friends with all three of the men that I asked to observe me, and I socialize with them all outside of school on occasion, so I knew they would be honest with me. Neil coaches track and was not a bad track athlete himself. He has a daughter that is my daughter's age, and the girls are friends. I get to socialize with Neil's family outside of school because of the friendship between our daughters. Gary is a very involved teacher, and he was very helpful to me during my times of struggle. Gary was once named Teacher of the Year, so I welcomed and appreciated his aid. Mitch is a town councilman. I do not know where he finds the time to do that, teach, *and* coach tennis – which he does extremely well.

The general conclusion from Neil, Gary, and Mitch was that I was doing okay, but I was not the teacher that

I was before I got sick eight years ago. It made me realize that perhaps there *was* something to what the principal had been saying. I just never would have guessed that from the positive feedback I had been getting from students and parents.

But I did not want to be an "okay" teacher. I wanted to be a *great* teacher. That is what I was used to and what I expected from myself. However, I also had to admit to myself that I was concerned with my mental clarity. Occasionally I would forget to request photocopies I needed, or I would occasionally misplace copies that I had received. A couple of times I also misplaced assignments that students had already turned in. This did not seem fair to the students.

I prayed for wisdom and I talked to Karen about what I should do. I finally called a meeting with the principal and told him that I think that I should go on full disability. He agreed. Nine months of stress was immediately lifted off of me. It is amazing that I, Mr. Worry-About-Everything, am completely at peace with all of this, and even at peace with how our finances will be affected by my being on disability. But I am sure God is in control and I can relax in knowing that He is, and I am excited to see what He has in store for me next.

The principal threw a very nice going-away party for me. Many co-workers attended and said their goodbyes. It was nice to have that kind of support and encouragement. I was especially touched by the goodbye that I received from the athletic director's secretary, Marcy. The first time I met Marcy was my first year of teaching. In the summer of 1994, I had ridden on RAGBRAI (Register's All-Great Bike Ride Across Iowa). Marcy was from a town that I had passed through on the bike ride in that summer of 1994. Marcy thought that she recognized me and asked me if I had been on RAGBRAI that summer. When I said that I had been, her next question was inevitable. She asked, "Did you go down a beer slide?" That was in my younger, rebellious, "do anything to draw attention to myself" years, but even though I was embarrassed, I had to admit to this more mature woman that I did indeed go down the beer slide. From that moment, Marcy and I developed a friendly relationship. At the going-away party, with tears welding up in her eyes, Marcy gave me a hug, said goodbye, and gave me a nice card. In the card she had said that I was the best wrestling coach that she had ever worked with. Honestly, I think she was referring to my personality, not necessarily my skills as a coach.

I also received very touching cards from students. Even a few students that I had taught in past years came into my classroom and gave me cards, saying some nice things like, "You were the best teacher that I ever had." I also received one card from a young man who had caused me some difficulties during the trimester. In the card, he told me that he was sorry. I appreciated that. My department members and even a university professor that I had worked with took me to lunch and gave me a gift card to Barnes and Noble. Even if the circumstances were not what I would have wished for, these kind words and actions were all appreciated and were a wonderful way to finish my teaching career. When I look back honestly at all that happened that I had thought was so unfair, I must say that I think the principal was a pretty nice guy after all, and he had endured stresses right alongside me. All in all, it was an extremely pleasant way to "retire" at age 37 from a workplace that left me with 15 years of great memories.

There is still one more great comment I heard, this time from one of my former wrestlers. Two of my wrestlers, Matt and Erik, had opened a new restaurant called Blackstone. One side of the restaurant is more or less a sports bar and the other side of the restaurant is a family restaurant with a great atmosphere. The two sides are separated by a wall, so there is no interference between the sides. These two young men are about 26 years old and I am very proud of both of them. When my family and I showed up at Blackstone, I was treated with favors that I did not expect. Matt gave my family a free appetizer and said, "The wrestling coach is in the house and deserves a free appetizer." Erik gave me a free dessert after dinner and reminded me of a story I had forgotten about.

I had coached Erik for three years before Mark was hired. Erik was struggling making weight one night for weigh-ins the next day. I took him to Carver Hawkeye arena, which is where the Hawkeyes wrestle, and worked out with him, getting him down to the weight he needed. Erik was impressed that I did this even after I was not coaching him anymore. At the time, I hadn't thought about the impact this might have on the young wrestler. I guess it is always important to realize the impact, good and bad, that our words and actions have on people.

Chapter 9

With or Without God?

In light of all of the difficult things that had been happening in my life, I have been and am surprisingly upbeat. I would rather suffer with Christ than not suffer without Him. I am a stronger witness since I have been stricken with this illness than I ever was without it. Perhaps it's because people want to hear what this "crippled guy" has to say.

The Bible says that we will suffer as Christians, one way or another. If we have an easy life, then we tend to get complacent and then we are no threat to Satan. I realize that God has greater plans than what we can imagine. He surprises us with good things. When I surprise Karen with flowers, gifts, or nice notes on any given day – not necessarily a special occasion – she is filled with happiness because she knows that I am thinking about her. When I surprise my daughter with any gift, I receive a similar response for similar reasons. Well, I feel the same way toward God and His many surprises for me.

When dealing with this illness, I frequently recall Scripture. For example, in 2 Corinthians 12:7-8, we read that the apostle Paul has pleaded with the Lord three times to take away the "thorn in my flesh." Paul tells us in verses 9 and 10:

> ⁹ But he said to me, *"My grace is sufficient for you, for my power is made perfect in weakness."* Therefore I will boast all the more gladly about my weaknesses, so that Christ's power may rest on me. ¹⁰ That is why, for Christ's sake, I delight in weaknesses, in insults, in hardships, in persecutions, in difficulties. For when I am weak, then I am strong.

Romans 8:28 is an oft-quoted verse from the New Testament, but we should always make sure to read from verse 28 all the way through the end of the chapter at verse 39. Romans 8:28 says, *"And we know that in all things God works for the good of those who love him…"* That does not say that good things *always* happen to those who love Him, but that good *will* come out of it. That verse reminds me of Joseph being sold into slavery by his brothers, then rising up to second-in-command in Egypt. What Joseph's brothers intended for harm, God used for good. (Genesis 50:20)

And with the many trials I still face, I come back again to James 1:2-4, which reads:

> ² "Consider it pure joy, my brother, whenever you face trials of many kinds,
> ³ because you know that the testing of your faith develops perseverance.
> ⁴ Perseverance must finish its work so that you may be mature and complete, not lacking anything."

I am not overwhelmed with joy that most days I struggle to walk or stand up without a walker, nor that some days I must use a wheelchair. But I am filled with joy in that I know God will use this situation for my good and to bring glory to Himself. I have not felt that kind of joy most of my life.

Second Corinthians 4:16-18 speaks of what true joy is, the kind of joy that I now have:

> ¹⁶ Therefore we do not lose heart. Though outwardly we are wasting away, yet inwardly we are being renewed day by day. ¹⁷ For our light and momentary troubles are achieving for us an eternal glory that far outweighs them all. ¹⁸ So we fix our eyes not on what is seen, but on what is unseen. For what is seen is temporary, but what is unseen is eternal.

People tell me that it does not seem fair that I am going through all of the physical ailments that I am facing. How can a wrestler, a weight lifter, and a coach be stricken with such an illness? How could God let this happen? First of all, you need not walk ten feet in the hospital in any direction to realize how many people are much worse off than most of us. Secondly, the question that I pondered when writing the song "Gethsemane" comes up again. The question is not "How can God let bad things happen to good people?" but "How can God let *good* things happen to *bad* people?" None of us are good. Not one of us.

I am a lustful, proud, "do as I wanna do" rebel. Some may say, "Well, that was in your past. You're a new man now." In the sense that Jesus is now my Lord and Savior, that is true. But Jesus said in the Beatitudes that if you have broken one part of the law, you have broken all of the law. Be it a lie, out-of-wedlock sex, taking the Lord's name in vain, or murder, these are all acts of breaking the law. Therefore, we are all guilty and deserving of condemnation. Would you call someone a just judge if they let a child molester or murderer go free without consequence because they were "sorry"? No! You would call that person a *terrible* judge. Why should we expect differently from God? We are all made in His own image. Since we are all guilty, we are all sinners, and so we all deserve justice.

Romans 3:23 reminds us of this: *"...for all have sinned*

and fall short of the glory of God." We are all sinners, and yet, as Paul reminds us in Romans 6:23: *"For the wages of sin is death, but the gift of God is eternal life in Jesus Christ our Lord."* Now *that* is true love! Even though I am a continuously rebellious sinner who throws God's laws back into His face, saying "I can do it myself," God gives me the free gift of eternal life and accepts me into His holy presence, demonstrating a love that I will never comprehend in my lifetime on earth. The catch is that I had to *accept* and *embrace* this free gift. In Revelation 3:20, Jesus says, **"I stand at the door and knock, if anyone hears my voice and opens the door, I will come in and eat with him, and he with me."** We must first open the door to our hearts and receive this free gift.

It really is that simple, folks! Why is it so difficult for people to understand how I could be so joyous about such an awesome gift? Yet people continue to reject this gift, and it breaks my heart. It also breaks God's heart. The consequences will be grave, but what is a just judge to do?

God has told mankind of His expectations and the consequences for not obeying Him. He will follow through on His word. As a teacher, if I told my students to turn in their homework or they would fail, you would think I was a responsible teacher. As a parent, if I told my daughter to clean up her toys or there would be no treats tonight, you would think I was a responsible parent. So why would people *not* expect this from our Holy Teacher, our Heavenly Father? He loves us beyond our comprehension. He is forgiving beyond what we deserve. This is why I have so much joy! Even if I were able to once again bench press 300 pounds or ride my bicycle on RAGBRAI this summer, it would not even compare to this gift of God's love and grace.

I absolutely love my life. My wife and my child are treasured blessings from God. I love them and I am grateful for them. I thank God for them every day. God made me, equipped me, and shaped me into the man that I am today through all sorts of experiences, including the one I am faced with today. It is for my good and it will bring Him glory. Living in vanity, self-indulgence, or just selfish pride is not only unimportant any longer, I finally recognize these things for what they are: disobedience to God, my Father. This is sin!

What I now recognize as important are my family, my friends, and obedience to God's will. These all involve healthy relationships, and all of us "growing up" in our relationship with God. Nothing else really matters. I am blessed, not in *spite* of my afflictions, but *because* of my afflictions. God's way is not man's way. So praise the Lord is all that I can really say. Join me now in saying, "Praise the Lord!" Amen.

Chapter 10

Wait on the Lord

But they that wait upon the LORD shall
renew their strength; they shall mount up
with wings as eagles; they shall run, and not
be weary; and they shall walk, and not faint.
– Isaiah 40:31 [King James Version]

It has been three years since the first edition of this
book was published, and four years since I handed the first
draft to my editor. I put off a new edition for a few years
because I thought the only updates would be regarding
my health, but God has made enough significant changes
that I thought it was time to go ahead and add this short
chapter to share His great work.

Since my original autobiography was published,
besides being confined mostly to a wheelchair, I have
all but lost my short-term memory. This memory loss is
quite taxing on my wife. It is frustrating for her to need

to repeat herself multiple times just five minutes after she just told me something. The short-term memory loss has been frustrating for me, too. Although I cannot play my guitar anymore, I still sing in the church praise band – but I can no longer learn new songs. I remember songs I learned prior to 2005, but I cannot learn new lyrics, and with my fading eyesight, I can't even read them. You see, I have not lost my long-term memory. That seems strange to me, but as the doctor explained to me, long and short-term memory deal with different parts of the brain.

As I just mentioned – and most frustrating to me – I am also drastically losing my vision. My left eye has been as bad as 20/400 (which is legally blind), and my right eye is 20/100. Even reading large print text is difficult, and I must listen to books and the Bible on tape or CD.

However, despite having lost my short-term memory and my eyesight, God shows me His awesomeness in that I am still able to memorize Scripture! I am up to one-hundred-seventy verses at my most recent count.

Like my father, I have also been diagnosed with Post-Traumatic Stress Disorder. Though I was never in a life-threatening war, apparently my own traumatic stress stems from my near-fatal car accident on January 26, 2001. I do still suffer anxiety whenever driving past a car in a ditch, or when riding in a car during snowy or icy conditions.

As my vision started to fade, I still continued to

carefully drive around town, having memorized routes to most places. But in 2010, while driving with my daughter for a "lunch date," I rear-ended a pickup truck, totaling both cars. My daughter got minor whiplash, but nobody was seriously hurt. Luckily, the man I hit was a good ol'-fashioned country farmer, with ol'-fashioned country values. He did not sue me, and in fact, right after the accident, instead of being angry, he consoled my weeping daughter. That was a gracious way for God to tell me not to drive again until He was ready to heal me.

I am not a patient man, historically, but I do realize that God's timing is not my timing. Second Peter 3:8 tells us that with God, a day is like a thousand years, and a thousand years is like a day. This is good for me to remember when I consider my illness and when God will restore my health. For now, I take joy in the fact that I have been a stronger, more effective witness for God from my wheelchair than I ever was out of it.

Back at the beginning of Chapter One, I mentioned that people ask me how I can love God through all of this, and it is a question I still get asked. Recently, I was listening to a sermon from Pastor Ajai Prakash about how some of the troubles of our lives are a result of the sin of our earlier days. That reminded me how God cursed the earth because of Adam and Eve's sin (Genesis 3:17-19), and so we have death and disease, and we must toil and sweat to tame this world so we can live. The consequences of past sin affect not only our own lives, but also our family and even our nation. Does that make God unlovable? I don't think so. I think it shows His justice in demanding that we repent, and it shows His mercy in that we have a chance to change our lives. My past carousing and promiscuity may very well be working itself out in my ailments today, but that is not God's fault, but mine. How can I not love a God who, despite my own past sin and doubt, allows me to live and glorify Him through my own life?

People also ask me, "Don't you miss playing guitar, driving, wrestling and coaching wrestling, playing and coaching soccer, and teaching?" My response is, "Of course I do. But I try not to focus on what I cannot do or do not have. Rather I focus on the blessings that I do have in my life. God has given me a beautiful wife and daughter, and I have been able to draw closer to God than ever before."

When my students used to ask me if God could do anything, I would, in a cavalier response, say, "Of course He can." I should have said that there are two things He cannot do: He cannot lie and cannot be anything other than good. Because of that, we know that His promises are true, and evil cannot abide in His presence. He is the living, just, and loving God.

I have learned that God is my refuge and my strength (Psalm 46:1); that His grace is sufficient for me (2nd Corinthians 12:9); that in all things God works for the good of those who love Him. (Romans 8:28) As I mentioned in the previous chapter, that passage from Romans doesn't say that only good things will happen to those who love God, but that the end result will be for their good. I have been a better witness for Jesus Christ in my wheelchair than I ever was as a singer, athlete, coach, or teacher. Besides writing this book, I also testify to God's love and power at events throughout our area. And I continue to have faith that I will be healed, because God also promises that all things are possible to him that believes. (Mark 10:27) So I am just waiting on the Lord, believing that when He is done with me growing up spiritually, He will completely restore me physically.

In Chapter 3 of the Gospel of John, Jesus has a conversation with a man named Nicodemus, who was a leader of the Jews. Nicodemus was a Pharisee and probably thought he had the whole "God thing" figured out, but he was still curious about the things Jesus was teaching and the miracles He performed. So Nicodemus came to Jesus and that was when Jesus told him that he needed to be born again, that being born of water (from the womb) was not enough. In order to see the kingdom of God, he needed to be born again of the Spirit, and that meant believing in Jesus as the Christ, the Anointed One, the only begotten Son of God. You see, God didn't send Jesus simply to teach us but to **save** us, to graciously die for our sins so that we can be, as He Himself said, *born again*. When we accept that Jesus died for us and that He lives again, we are born again into new life. Our old life of sin and guilt and regret is gone, and we are a new creation, a new brother or sister adopted into the family of God. In other words, even if we are like Nicodemus and think we know God, we don't truly know Him and we will not see Him or His kingdom until we are born again by accepting Jesus as our Lord and our Savior.

If you are not sure if you have accepted Jesus Christ as Lord and Savior, you had better get sure. Please, don't wait. Romans 10:9 says **"That if you confess with your mouth, 'Jesus is Lord,' and believe in your heart that God raised Him from the dead, you will be saved."** Once you have done that, then you'll begin a new life – and you'll get the chance to start growing up all over again.

Thank you, and may the blessings of God be with you all. Amen.

If you are interested in MP3s of my songs, they are available online at http://cdbaby.com/cd/troylangos.

CPSIA information can be obtained
at www.ICGtesting.com
Printed in the USA
FFOW04n1031240715
15388FF